For Eva McKenna

With my very best wishes

and thanks!

Nancy Henderson

November 17, 1972

WALK TOGETHER

Five Plays on Human Rights

By NANCY HENDERSON

Illustrated by Floyd Sowell

JULIAN MESSNER NEW YORK

Published by Julian Messner, a Division of Simon & Schuster, Inc.
1 West 39 Street, New York, N. Y. 10018. All rights reserved.

Copyright © 1972 by Nancy Henderson

For permission to perform these plays outside of the
classroom, please apply to the author's agents,
McIntosh and Otis, Inc., 18 East 41st Street,
New York, N. Y. 10017.

Printed in the United States of America

Design by Marjorie Zaum K.

BOOKS BY NANCY HENDERSON
Walk Together: Five Plays on Human Rights
The Scots Helped Build America

Library of Congress Cataloging in Publication Data

Henderson, Nancy Wallace.
  Walk Together: Five Plays on Human Rights.

  CONTENTS: The pledge.—Harvest for Lola.—Get on
board, little children. [etc.]
  [1. Plays. 2. Civil rights—Drama] I. Sowell,
Floyd, illus. II. Title.
PS3558.E489W3   812'.5'4   72-1423
ISBN 0-671-32537-X
ISBN 0-671-32538-8 (MCE)

ACKNOWLEDGMENTS

When I think of WALK TOGETHER, I see a great procession of those who walked with me. Most of them I can thank only in this way.

In researching THE PLEDGE on Apache reservations, I was welcomed in the homes of many Indians. I had much assistance from Nilla Hilborn of the Office of Economic Opportunity (OEO), Gertrude B. Van Roekel of the Bureau of Indian Affairs, and Cevero Caramillo, an Apache elder who led me into his hogan and showed me what living and dying mean to Jicarilla Apaches. At San Carlos I was given hospitality, information and introductions by Robert E. Hickman of OEO. My friend Britton Goode, a San Carlos Apache, supplied Apache names and pronunciations and checked the script for Indian authenticity. Katharine Taylor, principal of St. Luke's Parish School, New York City, teachers and fourth-grade students made possible a workshop production of THE PLEDGE.

Background material for HARVEST FOR LOLA was enriched by visits to Spanish-speaking migrant workers near Bridgeton, New Jersey. This was arranged through Jose Reyes (Caesar Chavez' troubleshooter in Jersey City), OEO lawyer Max D. Rothman and social workers Sandra Carbonell and Marta Benavides.

For the documentary form of GET ON BOARD, LITTLE CHILDREN, I am indebted to Arthur Arent's play, ONE THIRD OF A NATION, a Federal Theater Broadway hit in 1938. Bertha Johnson and Matilda Gutman, drama consultants of the Bank Street At Harlem project, produced this play at P.S. 9 and P.S. 180, New York City, with loving cooperation from teachers and children.

Efforts of Hannah Weiner, psychodramatist, and Theodore R. Smith, Jr., psychotherapist, stretched the imagination of the author and made LOOK BEHIND THE MASK a different, more meaningful play. Ann Guenther and her students at the Friends Seminary School were helpful in testing the script in class.

I was introduced to the teaching machines involved in AUTOMA by Etta Dinerstein of New York City School Volunteers. Joseph Schumacher, principal of P.S. 198, New York City, obtained pertinent comments on the plays from his teachers.

Valuable criticism and suggestions on the entire project were given by Benjamin Bernard Zavin, playwright and teacher, and the following writers, friends and relatives: Edward Bartley, Richard de Long, Jane Dewey, Charlotte Kraft, Barbara Lucas, Barbara Nadolny, William Henderson, Charles Jennings and Penny Sisson. And much help and support have been given me by my editor, Lee Hoffman, her educational consultant, Doris Coburn, and her assistants at Julian Messner.

Walter Zervas, of the Research Library Administration Office, New York Public Library, made available the privacy and convenience of the Frederick Lewis Allen Room for my research of the historical data on which these plays are based.

Nancy Henderson

CONTENTS

For a' that and a' that
It's comin yet for a' that
That man to man the warld o'er
Shall brothers be for a' that.

—Robert Burns

To Bill
With Love Ongoing

These plays are about the struggles of human beings for their human rights—freedom and equality for all people. The United States is a country that was founded on such ideals. The Declaration of Independence speaks of "unalienable rights of life, liberty, and the pursuit of happiness." And the Constitution of the United States proclaims the right of all persons to freedom of speech, assembly, the press; freedom from slavery; the right to a speedy trial, the right to vote, to attend all schools, own property, and hold any job. These are also called civil rights.

As citizens of the United States, we believe one of the duties of our government is to protect the human rights of all our people—especially against any kind of tyranny. But the cruel or unjust use of power takes away the rights of some of the people. The Constitution was written to protect everyone from tyranny, and laws have been passed to carry out these aims. Sometimes people in power find ways of getting around the laws so that they are not always enforced. And some laws against human rights have actually been passed.

Many Americans have lived and died without achieving their human rights. They have had their religion declared unlawful. They have been bought and sold by other men. They have been refused the right to bargain for a living wage. They have been jailed and sometimes killed for trying to take for themselves the rights our Constitution guarantees.

Recently a group of school children made up a list of human rights for all children. Here are some of them: All races should have equal rights; all children have a right to be loved and cared for, to choose their own religion, to live in a peaceful world, to be treated fairly, to have some part in making decisions that affect them, to think and express their own ideas and opinions. What would your list be?

Giving a play is an exciting way of learning. The plays in this book show glimpses of the courage of Americans striving to gain some of the rights denied them, in the past and present.

THE PLEDGE, which is a story about American Indians, is based on historical fact. From it you will learn of the desperate efforts of Apaches to stay alive after their military defeat, and to keep their tribal way of life from being destroyed. This is their *right to live and be themselves.* In the play, the tribe finds a way to the future by making a decision of its own.

HARVEST FOR LOLA is also based on facts in our time. It shows how hard it is for migrant workers to feed and educate their children. Some people in government do not understand how much these children hate being uprooted from their schools and moved on to another community, just when they are beginning to learn and make friends. In this play, Lola is fighting for the *right to learn.*

GET ON BOARD, LITTLE CHILDREN is a history play about a simple right we take for granted—the *right of a person to be free,* not owned by any other person. Today, it is hard for us to realize that men could once buy and sell one another. Yet a little over a hundred years ago, unjust and cruel laws in our country allowed this to happen. Here the true events of the abolition of slavery in the United States and the Underground Railroad are acted out on stage. This is a documentary play, and its own introduction tells you more about what that means. Documentaries used to be called "living newspapers" because the scenes were news about real happenings in our world.

LOOK BEHIND THE MASK shows how the "masks" we sometimes wear make us appear what we are not, and how we can learn to know and understand one another. This is a play about getting rid of the masks—the *right to like your real self, and be liked.*

AUTOMA reminds us that people are always more important than the machines they invent. This play gives an idea of what might happen to children if they should lose the *right to think and make decisions.*

PRODUCTION

These plays are intended to be used in many ways. Try them out freely in your schoolrooms and clubs. It does not matter whether you use a stage. Each play should be produced as simply as possible, for that is the way they will work best. If they are staged in daytime, they can be done without lighting. If you want to darken your auditorium or plan an evening production, lights will add much to the effect. Feel free to change lines or scenes, or to make up lines of your own. You will find production notes at the end of each play, to help you with the staging. The size of the cast can be changed to suit your needs, so that every one in your class or group can have a part.

REHEARSAL

When rehearsals begin, *do not try to read from the script at first.* Learn the story of the play and what it means, and take turns telling parts of it in your own words. Then get up and begin to act it out, *making up your own lines* and thinking about what your character is like. This will make the play and your own part come alive for you. After you have been through the whole play this way enough times to feel that you know what it is about, then try a rehearsal with the script, reading your lines as you walk through the action. Now you may want to take turns, using your own made-up lines at one rehearsal and then using the script at the next. You will find yourself remembering more and more lines from the script as you go on. Memorizing your part should come last, after you feel well acquainted with the character you are acting and the whole play. A pronunciation guide will be found wherever names or words are strange to you.

Lines marked "all speak at once" should be said just that way, everyone interrupting everyone else. By dividing your group into sections and giving a signal for all to talk at once, you can make this sound like real crowd noises.

The playing time is given at the end of each play. As you come closer to the date set for your production, start timing each run-through and begin to work on tempo, which means the rate of speed at which the play is acted. A fast tempo makes for a lively performance that will interest the audience. You should be able to reach the suggested playing time if you strive towards this.

STAGE DIRECTIONS

The terms "stage right" and "stage left" are used to direct the *actors,* so that when they stand *facing the audience,* stage right is on their right, and stage left on their left. "Upstage" means toward the back, and "downstage" is down front.

When you are asked to "pantomime" a door or a prop, this means to act it with gestures so that you make the audience believe it is there. For example, when you pantomime a "door," you must make sure that people "opening" it go to the same spot each time and put out their hands to turn the "knob" at the same place and height. It is surprising how much the audience will see and believe if this is done carefully. It also adds to the excitement of your staging.

All of the plays will work better with simple staging, letting the action of the play do most of the job. You do not need a curtain at all. Often it gets in the way and makes the audience feel cut off from you. If you feel that you must use the curtain, keep it for the beginning and ending only. Never use it to break the action during the play. If your auditorium has no backstage space for entrances and exits, you don't have to follow the stage directions exactly where groups are told to go offstage. They can stay on, standing motionless at the back at times when they are not supposed to be in the scene. Or they can simply come down into the auditorium at the side of the stage and sit quietly until time to enter again.

THE PLEDGE

The Apaches were wanderers who came down from the northern part of America and settled in the Southwest. They had very few contacts with other tribes. They did not weave blankets or rugs or make jewelry. They never settled down to farm or herd sheep or cattle until the reservations were formed. They were horsemen and hunters who fought with bows and arrows, and raided other tribes and white settlers for their food. They were brave and proud, and they lived for glory.

When the United States Army finally conquered the Apaches, they were confined to reservations by the government. A Bureau of Indian Affairs was set up in Washington to protect Indian rights. But the white politicians controlled the Bureau, and Indians were mistreated more often than protected. The white man thought of himself as the true American. By destroying everything Indian, he intended to make the Indians like himself. That is why Indian children were sent away to boarding schools and were cut off from every contact with their families.

Powerful white cattlemen in the Southwest convinced the United States Army and government that they needed the land for their herds. They forced the Apaches to sign away parts of their reservations and to lease them the rest of the good grazing land. There was scarcely enough fertile land left for raising crops, and they had no way of working for a living. This meant idleness for the Indians and surviving on scanty government rations. Many Apaches sickened and died of tuberculosis. By 1920, their death rate was higher than their birth rate. They seemed truly doomed to vanish from the earth.

But the tide was turned, with the help of a few white men who determined to fight the injustice and cruelty. The Indians had always thought of the land as a sacred gift from the Creator, for the use of all men. But when the white man took it, Indians had to cope with their conquerors' laws on property rights in order to defend themselves. So Apaches learned how to cancel the unfair leases, and began to raise cattle on their own land. They cared nothing for this kind of life, but saw it as a way to survive in the white man's world. Herding cattle was active and out of doors. And it was an opportunity to use Apache land for the profit of the tribe.

Apaches began to govern themselves once again in tribal councils. They demanded that their children be taught on the reservation, and that the government provide better health services. By 1934, tuberculosis was almost entirely conquered.

Today, the American Indian is still struggling for his right to live as an Indian, and to live his own life fully, without want. He is becoming more and more himself. Many white Americans at last are beginning to recognize the mistakes that were made in the past and the needless suffering that was caused. This play, based on history, is the story of Apaches living in the early 1900s, and how they met the challenge of these years.

CHARACTERS

(The column on the right side tells you how to pronounce the names. The Apache language does not accent syllables. If there are two vowels together, you hold the vowel sound. If there is only one vowel, say it quickly. If it has marks over it, you raise your voice on that syllable. If it has a mark under it, you say it "through your nose.")

JAADE, a tribal elder	jaah-duh
TALKALAÍ, the chief	tuck-lie
YOO', a woman of the tribe	yo-ah
LEVITT, a white cattleman	
JACKSON, a white cattleman	
DAVIS, a white cattleman	
JONES, a white cattleman	
NACHEE, a young leader	nah-chy
NAATÚ, wife of NACHEE	naah-toe
CHATO, their son	chah-toe
HIDLO'H, their daughter	hid-lo
DAWOO, a tribal elder	dah-wo
MA'CHO'K, a tribal elder	mah-cho-keh
BUCK, a soldier	
SLIM, a soldier	
JARVIS, the white superintendent	
KA'A	kah
CHAA	chah
GAH CH'O } Indian children	gah choke
ITSÁ	it-sah
BACHI	baah-chy

The scene is an outdoor gathering place on an Apache Indian reservation. It is an autumn day, about the year 1920. Upstage left is a wickiup (wi-ki-up), an Apache dwelling.

(The CHORUS, *all of the Apaches, moves in a dance step across the stage, stopping up right. Some of them are*

beating skin-covered drums; others dance with bows and arrows. The men are dressed in buckskin vests and trousers, the women in blouses and long skirts. All wear headbands. JAADE, *a tribal elder, comes forward and speaks to the audience, looking into their faces like a storyteller.)*

JAADE.   I am Jaade, an Apache Indian. We Apaches lived in America long years before the white man came. *(He moves right, stands at edge of stage.)*

(The CHORUS *comes downstage. They divide into three groups for* CHORUS *lines, with all speaking at once, loudly and quickly, to make a clamor.)*

CHORUS. *(Group 1)*   Yes—long before.
(Group 2)   Long years before.   *(All speak*
(Group 3)   Long, long years.   *at once.)*

*(*TALKALAÍ *steps forward. He wears a buckskin shirt, leggings, moccasins, a breech cloth, a skin cap, and a headdress of feathers. His bearing is very proud.)*

TALKALAÍ.   I am Talkalaí, the chief of the tribe. We were all great runners, hunters, and brave fighters with our bows and arrows.

(The drums beat as YOO', *a woman of the tribe comes downstage.)*

YOO'.   But many white men came with guns and fought us.

TALKALAÍ.   Finally they won, but we knew they could never equal us, man for man.

CHORUS.   (1) Never, never could equal us.

(2) No, they could never equal us.   *(All speak*
(3) Never, man for man.   *at once.)*

JAADE.   After the fighting ended, the white men took away the best of our land and drove us out of it, with their guns.

(LEVITT, JACKSON, DAVIS, and JONES, four white cattlemen, dressed in jeans, western shirts and boots, carrying revolvers, enter from left. Brandishing their guns, they advance on the Apaches, forcing them upstage. LEVITT draws an imaginary circle around the Indians.)

LEVITT.   From now on, you must live on this reservation. The land will belong to you. Boundary here.

TALKALAÍ.   Why a boundary? The land is free.

(Drums beat. Apaches dance slowly within the boundary. The cattlemen form a huddle, shaking their heads, whispering.)

DAVIS.   Look here, we need more land for our own herds.

(The cattlemen push the Apaches farther upstage. LEVITT draws a smaller circle.)

CHORUS *(protesting)*. (1) No, no, no.
(2) You promised we would live here.
(3) This is not what you promised.
(All speak at once.)

JONES.   Tell you what—we'll pay you rent for the land.

TALKALAÍ *(angrily)*.   What is this rent? There is room for all.

(The cattlemen push the protesting Apaches farther

upstage right, then form a guard around the smaller boundary line, their backs to the audience.)

JAADE. Now they graze all their cattle on the land they said was for us. And they take our children away from their mothers. The white men took this young brave, Nachee, when he was only six years old, to live in their school, many miles from here. *(He beckons to* NACHEE, *who comes down right beside him. The cattlemen go off. The Apaches come downstage.)*

NACHEE. I did not see my family again until I was sixteen. For ten years the white people tried to make me forget I was Apache. They told me an Indian could be *just as good* as a white man! *(*CHORUS *laughs loudly.)* This happened to many Apache children.

JAADE *(pointing to* NACHEE*).* When Nachee came back, he was a stranger to us.

TALKALAÍ *(nodding).* He had forgotten how to talk in Apache.

NACHEE. But I learned much in that school—and I learned about white people. I dreamed of teaching Apache children here—but we had no school on the reservation. Then I married Naatú. *(*NAATÚ, *a young Apache woman, and* CHATO *and* HIDLO'H, *a boy and girl, come and stand beside him.)* This is Naatú, and these are our children. After they were born, I became a guide for hunters.

DAWOO *(mockingly).* He works for the white men.

MA'CHO'K. Takes them hunting in the hills.

NACHEE. They pay me well. I must earn a living for my family.

(NACHEE goes off down right, followed by the jeering CHORUS.)

JAADE. Nachee has learning. Perhaps someday he could be our chief.

TALKALAÍ. First he must win the trust of his people.

(TALKALAÍ goes off right. NAATÚ, CHATO, and HIDLO'H are alone on stage. They are moving toward the wickiup when two white soldiers, BUCK and SLIM, enter from down left.)

JAADE. One time, when Naatú really needed him, Nachee was far away hunting.

(The soldiers stand on either side of CHATO, who looks as if he wants to run away, but sees it is too late.)

BUCK. All right, kid, let's go for a ride.

NAATÚ *(alarmed)*. He is not going anywhere.

SLIM. It's school time, pretty squaw. Don't you want your little brave to learn to read and write?

NAATÚ. You cannot take him—his father is away. *(to HIDLO'H)* Go and find Talkalaí! *(HIDLO'H runs off right.)*

BUCK. His father's away? That's the best time, then.

(SLIM grasps CHATO firmly, pins his arms behind him, walks him left. CHATO struggles and cries out. NAATÚ wrestles with the soldier fiercely, trying to free CHATO.)

SLIM. Guess we'll have to take Squaw Mama to the lockup. *(SLIM grasps NAATÚ's arms. NAATÚ screams.)* She can cool off overnight.

(The soldiers drag CHATO *and* NAATÚ *off left, both struggling and shouting.)*

HIDLO'H. Talkalaí cannot help—he has fallen ill with the coughing sickness.

*(*NAATÚ *runs on from left, weeping.* HIDLO'H *enters from right, meets* NAATÚ *at center, comforts her. Apaches begin to drift back onstage.)*

JAADE. Our land and our children are taken away—our people are sick and starving. Our hope has come to an end. *(He looks up, raises his arms.)* Great Father, help us!

(Drums beat softly. Led by JAADE, *the* CHORUS *moves in rhythm. They sing.)*

CHORUS *(singing)*. Oh, Great Father,
We ask you to help us
Fill us with strength
Lest we grow faint
Hear us, Great Spirit
In all our need
Our flame of hope
Burns very low
Send us much rain
Corn that grows tall
Give us good hunting
Deer in the forest
Give us your help
Good friend of man.

(The CHORUS *dances slowly off right at the end of the prayer.* NAATÚ *and* HIDLO'H *follow.* JAADE *remains on stage, steps forward.)*

JAADE. After two moons, Nachee returned to an angry wife.

*(*NAATÚ *and* NACHEE *enter together from right.)*

NAATÚ.   Where were you when the soldiers dragged my Chato away?

NACHEE.   Naatú, I didn't know. I would have killed anyone who laid a hand on you or Chato.

JAADE.   That would only bring more soldiers and bloodshed among our people.

NACHEE.   If it had to be, I think Chato will benefit from the white man's teaching. He will learn to defend himself and help his tribe.

*(*TALKALAÍ *enters slowly from right, leaning on a cane.)*

NAATÚ *(to* NACHEE*).*   You learned all that, and it did not help.

TALKALAÍ.   We need his learning now. *(to* NACHEE*)* The Apaches have a new superintendent. His name is Jarvis. He has come from the Bureau of Indian Affairs in Washington to sell our land. He says he will get us a good price.

NACHEE.   This buying and selling of land is the white man's idea. We have a treaty . . .

JAADE *(smiling sadly).*   When did we not have treaties?

TALKALAÍ.   Our people are dying from the coughing sickness. The treaty says when all of the tribe is dead, the government takes back the land.

NACHEE.   The white men have doctors and hospitals . . .

JAADE.   No good ones for us.

NACHEE.   Let me go and see Mr. Jarvis.

JAADE. How can you speak for the Apaches? You think like a white man now.

TALKALAÍ. He knows how to talk to the white man. *(to* NACHEE *)* Go, and speak for the tribe. *(Suddenly faint,* TALKALAÍ *falls back into* JAADE's *arms as* NACHEE *goes off left.)* I am tired. I must go to my wickiup.

NAATÚ. You are ill, Talkalaí. I will look for the roots for your medicine.

(JAADE *helps* TALKALAÍ *off right.* NAATÚ *begins to dig among the rocks upstage. Suddenly* HIDLO'H *and* CHATO *steal on from right, looking around to see if they are being followed.* NAATÚ *turns, cries out for joy.)*

NAATÚ. Chato—you have come back!

*(*CHATO *runs to her.)*

HIDLO'H. He ran away from the school!

NAATÚ. How did you find us, my son?

CHATO. I remembered the long trail—and asked people how to go.

NAATÚ. Did anyone follow you?

CHATO. No, I hid from the police. They caught one boy who ran away. They brought him back and whipped him, and made him wear girls' clothes. Everybody laughed at him.

HIDLO'H. You have lost your amulet, Chato. *(She fingers hers, which is hanging around her neck.)* You were supposed to wear it night and day.

CHATO. They took it away from me. We can't wear anything Indian in that school.

NAATÚ *(her eyes flashing angrily).* You are not going back there. *(She looks him over.)* You are dirty and covered with scratches.

CHATO. I'm very hungry.

NAATÚ. You will have some food in the wickiup and go to sleep.

CHATO *(pointing offstage right).* I found a horse on the prairie. See, I tied him to that tree. He brought me many miles today. His coat is like gold. *(*NAATU *and* HIDLO'H *look.)*

HIDLO'H. Gold like the grass after it is cut for thatching.

NAATÚ *(looking off left).* I see your father coming this way with Mr. Jarvis. Quick, go into the wickiup.

*(*NAATÚ, CHATO, *and* HIDLO'H *go inside.* NACHEE *enters from left, followed by* JARVIS, *a white man wearing a plaid shirt and khaki trousers.)*

JARVIS. The cattlemen are coming here to talk to you, Nachee. They think you will understand what they want.

NACHEE. I understand how they are getting rich, Mr. Jarvis, grazing their cattle on the best land, the places they guard with their guns.

JARVIS. Didn't the tribe sign leases? You agreed to rent them your grazing land.

NACHEE. What does a lease mean, Mr. Jarvis? There was plenty of land for all. These leases were papers that tricked us. Some Apaches couldn't read English, and the

whites lied about what was written on them. Sometimes
they got our people drunk to make them sign. The papers
were to keep us from walking on the land. And the rent
was not enough to pay for our food.

JARVIS.   If I sell it for you, I'll see that you get a good price.

NACHEE.   Money in a large pile slips away like dry sand.
Could you help us to do away with these leases, Mr.
Jarvis?

JARVIS.   Does your tribe have any cattle, Nachee?

NACHEE.   Talkalaí and the elders have a small, half-starved
herd.

JARVIS.   Would you use the land—fatten your cattle and
breed more?

NACHEE (hesitating).   My people have no love for herding
cattle . . .

JARVIS.   Still it's better than no work at all. If I go against
the white men, I'll be risking my job. I'd like to have your
word that the Apaches would use this land.

NACHEE.   I cannot speak for the tribe. They have been
cheated so many times, they may not believe me.

(LEVITT, JACKSON, DAVIS, and JONES enter from down
right.)

LEVITT.   Nachee, we want to talk to you.

JONES.   We hear the Apaches are dying so fast, they're
burning a wickiup every day.

JACKSON.   Now the government wants to sell us your land.

NACHEE. The Apaches do not sell what belongs to all.

DAVIS. Are you speaking for the tribe now, Nachee?

NACHEE. I am speaking for Talkalaí, the Chief.

JARVIS. The Apaches live under the white man's law now, Nachee. The cattlemen will pay a good price.

JONES. Not too fast, Jarvis. Remember the Apaches are enemies of this country—lucky to get paid anything.

NACHEE *(coldly)*. Summers and winters make fifty rounds since we fought with you. And the land you took was a free gift from the Great Father for the use of all men.

LEVITT. You Apaches don't know how to use it.

NACHEE. When we had the land, we loved and cared for it better than you do. *(to* JARVIS*)* Mr. Jarvis, you are here to represent the Apaches.

JARVIS. That's right, Nachee.

JACKSON. Mr. Jarvis is new around here. He's going to find out pretty fast who the bosses are.

NACHEE. Mr. Jarvis works for us, in the Bureau of Indian Affairs.

(The cattlemen laugh hard at this.)

JONES. Sure. Those boys in the Bureau—we're the ones got 'em their jobs, Nachee.

NACHEE. I have heard that some of them are our friends. Do they know how little rent the tribe is getting, Mr. Jarvis?

JARVIS *(nodding)*. They know it's not enough.

JACKSON *(angrily)*. It's all you're going to get, unless you agree to sell. Tell the old chief that from me, Nachee.

LEVITT. As for you, Jarvis—you better soft-pedal that stuff about us paying big prices. All we gotta do is write a couple of letters to Washington, and you'll be on your way out of here.

(The cattlemen swagger off right.)

JARVIS. We won't let them frighten us, Nachee. Talk to the tribe—let me know what they decide. *(He goes off left.)*

NACHEE *(staring after him)*. The tribe does not trust me—do I dare to trust a white man?

*(*CHATO *puts his head out of the wickiup.)*

NACHEE. Chato! What are you doing here?

*(*CHATO *steps out, runs to his father, who puts an arm around him.* NAATÚ *and* HIDLO'H *follow.)*

NAATÚ. He has run away from school—and he isn't going back. They are not kind to him in that school.

NACHEE *(smiling at* CHATO*)*. Little brave, you will be the talk of the reservation.

HIDLO'H *(alarmed)*. The soldiers must not find him here.

CHATO. No, no. I would run away into the hills first, and die with my horse.

NAATÚ. And I would go and die with you. Go to sleep now.

*(*CHATO *goes back into the wickiup.* JAADE *comes on from right, stands with arms folded to make his announcement.)*

JAADE.   Now Talkalaí is dying. The women are singing the songs of healing, but his spirit struggles to leave his body. He sends for Nachee.

> (NACHEE, NAATÚ, *and* HIDLO'H *go off right. Drumbeats are heard faintly in the distance.* CHATO *steals out of the wickiup and looks around. He is starting off left when a group of Apache children run to meet him. They stalk him around the stage, teasing him.*)

KA'A.   There is Chato, son of Nachee.

CHAA.   You went away to school, Chato, the white man's school.

GAH CH'O.   Chato's father is the white man's friend.

ITSÁ.   Chato's not Apache any more.

CHATO.   I am Apache. I ran away from school.

JAADE.   What are you going to do, Chato? They'll send you back.

CHATO.   They won't find me—unless you tell.

CHAA.   Oh, we don't talk to white men—we never went to school.

GAH CH'O.   That your pretty horse, tied up over there?

KA'A.   They won't let you keep it. Watch, a white man will take that horse!

CHATO.   No one's going to take my horse. We will both be gone.

ITSÁ.   They'll find you, Chato. You're not good at hiding.

CHATO. They won't find me—I'm going to the hills!

(CHATO runs off right. The children follow him to the edge of the stage, calling, "Chato, Chato!" BUCK and SLIM, the soldiers, come on from left.)

BUCK. Hey, kids, we're looking for a little boy named Chato.

BACHI *(stepping back warily).* Chato—Nachee's son?

GAH CH'O. He was sent away to school.

SLIM. Yeah, but I think I saw him here today, walking a horse—a palomino.

ITSÁ. Chato is far away. Must have been somebody else.

(All the children nod.)

BUCK. If you do see him, let us know.

(They nod pleasantly.)

KA'A. Sure, sure. If we see him, we'll let you know.

(The soldiers go off left. The children move up right, where the elders and CHORUS are coming onstage. NACHEE, NAATÚ, and HIDLO'H move toward the wicki-up just as CHATO runs on from left, followed by JACK-SON, who holds him firmly by the arm. CHATO is straining to get away. JARVIS and the soldiers follow.)

CHATO. Father, this man took my horse. Tell him I found that horse—he belongs to *me*.

NACHEE *(to JACKSON).* Take your hands off my son. *(to CHATO)* Chato, you would have been safe in the wickiup.

JACKSON (*letting go of* CHATO). I passed the kid on the road. He was running away—figured he stole the horse.

CHATO. I didn't steal him. I found him. He's mine, I tell you.

JACKSON. I'll pay him a couple of bucks for that horse.

JAADE (*stepping forward*). The white man cannot have the horse.

(*The* CHORUS *comes downstage.*)

CHORUS. (1) White man, you cannot have
           the horse.
        (2) You get out of here.   (*All speak at once.*)
        (3) Get off the reservation.

JARVIS. I reckon that settles it, Mr. Jackson.

JACKSON (*backing away as the Apaches close in*). Just making a business deal . . .

CHORUS (*laughing*). (1) Yes, yes—two bucks!
                     (2) Big deal.   (*All speak
                     (3) Big business deal.   at once.*)

(*Apaches chase* JACKSON *off left, shaking their fists.*)

NACHEE. The cattlemen will not rest now, Mr. Jarvis, until your footprints are gone.

JARVIS. I'm not afraid of them, Nachee.

DAWOO. That's right, Jarvis, why be afraid? Why don't you go with Jackson?

CHORUS. (1) Yes—let Jarvis go.
       (2) Jarvis, too.   *(All speak at once.)*
       (3) Jarvis, go with Jackson.

NACHEE. Apaches, I beg you not to turn against a friend. You heard Mr. Jarvis take my son's part.

MA'CHO'K. Nachee sides with the white men. Let him go, too.

CHORUS. (1) Nachee, too.
       (2) Nachee is not Apache.   *(All speak*
       (3) Let Nachee go with the white   *at once.)*
          men.

JAADE *(raising his voice, silences them).* Tribesmen, our chief is dead. In the midst of mourning, we must decide what path to take. We must choose a new chief.

DAWOO. It should be you, Jaade.

JAADE *(shaking his head).* I am old, Dawoo. It should be a young man. And Nachee was our great chief's choice.

CHORUS *(jeering).* (1) Nachee?
             (2) The white man's   *(All speak*
                helper?   *at once.)*
             (3) Nachee our chief?

MA'CHO'K. Jaade, you can see the tribe does not trust Nachee.

JAADE. That is foolish, Ma'cho'k. Nachee is working for us.

The stage can be made to look like an outdoor meeting place by putting bushes or branches of trees around it. Stumps and rocks can be made out of wooden packing boxes covered with papier-mâché, shaped and painted. If your playing space has a light backdrop, use it to look like a sky. Against it fasten outlines of distant mountains cut out of cardboard. Your librarian or teacher can help you find illustrations of wickiups, Apache dress, and articles made and used by Apaches. The wickiup is the Apache's own dwelling and can be built on your stage with poles and pieces of cloth. It is a kind of tepee, but must be rounded at the top. Costumes made from brown cambric, or any other cotton material with a shiny finish, fringed with the same cloth, will resemble buckskin shirts, skirts, or trousers. Or the Indians can wear ordinary clothing of the time, with headbands. Perhaps you can find an Indian costume with a feather headdress for the chief.

In the music of the American Indians, the notes seem to be a little above or below the ones in the European scale. Most Indian tunes start high and come down to a low note at the end. Philip Cassadore's record, "Apache," Canyon Record ARP 6053 (Canyon Records, 834 N. 7th Ave., Phoenix, Arizona), gives the true sounds of Apache singing. Drums should be the kind that have a soft leather or skin covering. Here is a simple tune that can be used for humming at the opening of the play and for the prayer:

Oh — Great Fa—ther,   we   ask you to help us

If your stage has wings (backstage space on either side), the chorus can go on and off according to the directions. If not, they may remain onstage by standing at the back, motionless, when they are not supposed to be in the scene.

The number of Indian children depends on the number of people in your cast. If you want to add more, you can find names for them in books about the Apaches.

HARVEST FOR LOLA

Each year, the great farmlands of the United States produce crops that need many extra hands for the harvest. The pickers are called "migrant" workers because they "migrate," or move with their families from one place to another. They gather where apples, melons, or grapes are ripe, where fields are white from bursting cotton bolls, or where green beans hang from vines and bushes.

Many black, white, and Puerto Rican migrants call Florida "home base" because its warm climate produces crops during most of the year. In late April, workers travel from Florida to Virginia to harvest spring crops, and then move to New York or New Jersey, where other Puerto Ricans and some Mexican Americans also work. They may go as far north as Maine, and then back to Virginia for the September harvest, returning to Florida for the winter. In summer in southern California, Mexican Americans work their way north from county to county as each crop ripens.

Migrant workers sometimes make fairly good hourly wages, in addition to overtime pay, during the harvest. At that time they also put their children to work, some of whom are as young as nine. But in the weeks and months between crops, they earn nothing. The grower has always paid whatever he wished. In the 1960s, the average income for a migrant worker was between $900 and $1,200 a year, the lowest of any laborer in this country.

Cesar Chavez, a Mexican American, has succeeded in forming the first national union for farm workers. It is called the National Farm Workers Association (N.F.W.A.) and was organized in September, 1965, to support a strike for higher wages for grape pickers in California. The strike grew into a boycott of grapes in stores throughout the United States. After five years of struggle, the union was recognized and contracts were signed with grape growers for better pay and working conditions. The N.F.W.A. eagle stamp is now a sign everywhere that farm crops have been picked and are being sold under union contract. N.F.W.A. covers a small but growing group of workers who still must battle their way for every gain. But the eagle means hope for the migrant worker.

Very few migrants have homes of their own. Most of them live in labor camps built by the government or growers. Many of these camps are worse than a city slum. Often a large family lives in one room, with no bathroom or running water. Children play barefoot in garbage and filth outside.

Migrant children go to school for a few weeks or months until they have to move. Though it is against the law, their parents sometimes keep them out of school to work in the fields. Deadly pesticides are sprayed on crops to kill insects, and sometimes these sprays have hurt and killed workers. And strikers have been attacked and injured while picketing.

The children are often eager to learn, but they are too proud to come to school without proper clothing. Because they move around so much, it is hard for them to keep up with their studies and feel that they really belong. They need friends, encouragement, and education that can help them to a better life.

This play is about a Mexican American family that found out how much learning meant to their daughter, Lola.

CHARACTERS

(The column on the right side tells you how to pronounce the Spanish names. The syllable in capital letters is accented.)

STAGE MANAGER

LOLA	LO-lah
ELENA	el-AY-nah
JOSEFINA	ho-seh-FEE-na
SALVADOR	sahl-vah-DOR
CARLOS	KAHR-los
PANCHO	PAHN-cho
MRS. GARCÍA	gahr-SEE-ah
MR. GARCÍA	
SUSAN	
GAIL	
RUTH	
MIGUEL	mi-GEL
ALBERTO	ahl-BAIR-to
FRED	
DON	
CARMELITA	kahr-me-LEE-tah
FOREMAN	

PICKETS, SCHOOL CHILDREN

(Other Spanish names and words)

Julio	HOO-leo
La Causa	lah KOW-zah
Campesino	kahm-peh-SEE-no
Chicano	chi-KAH-no
Tortillas	tor-TEE-yahs
Anglos	AHNG-los

(Upstage is the room where the whole García family

lives, in a labor camp in southern California. The STAGE MANAGER *enters from right, carrying a sign which reads "Lola's Home."* STAGE MANAGER *goes off. Up right* MRS. GARCÍA *is sweeping.* SALVADOR, *seventeen, and* PANCHO, *fourteen, sit at a table reading comic books.* LOLA, *thirteen, has a rag which she dips in a basin of water on the table. She is washing the face of her sister,* ELENA, *who is ten.* JUANITA, *twelve, sits on a sagging cot covered with a grimy quilt, up center, putting on a pair of shoes.* JOSEFINA, *nine, lies on the cot, fingers pressing her stomach, moaning.* CARLOS, *eleven, is combing his long tangled hair. Gunny sacks around the floor mark places where the children sleep. A door leads outside, at right. It is the spring of 1968.)*

LOLA. Josefina, let me wash your face. Hurry, you'll be late for school.

JOSEFINA *(moaning loudly).* Lola, I have the stomach ache.

ELENA *(pressing her stomach, loudly).* So do I, Lola. Mine hurts very much.

LOLA. You were both feeling all right a minute ago.

ELENA. It's the spray—they sprayed the grapes, and it made me sick.

LOLA. Don't kid about that—it does make people sick. *(She crosses to* JOSEFINA, *wipes her face.)* Two years ago it killed our brother, Julio.

SALVADOR *(looking up, nods).* They forgot very fast.

LOLA. Carlos, you can't wear that shirt to school another day.

CARLOS.   I don't have a clean one.

LOLA.   Mama, you said you were going to wash . . .

MRS. GARCÍA.   You know how it rained yesterday. Nobody could wash. Maybe you should all take a day off.

LOLA.   We can't—we've just missed a whole week. *(She puts the rag and basin under the cot, looks around.)* Now, where are my shoes? *(The children giggle.)*

ELENA.   Look! Look at Juanita.

LOLA.   Juanita—you've got my shoes.

JUANITA.   They're too small for you, Lola. You've outgrown them.

JOSEFINA.   Let's go barefoot!

LOLA.   You know we can't go barefoot. The school won't allow it.

JUANITA *(slipping one off)*.   Here, Lola, I'll give them back.

LOLA *(looking under the cot)*.   No, you keep them. I think there's a pair in this box the church sent. *(She pulls out a pair and puts them on, tries to walk in them. They are too large.)*

ELENA.   Lola, they're crummy. They make you walk funny.

LOLA.   I can't help it.

JOSEFINA.   You don't care, just so you get to that old school.

SALVADOR.   Lola is right. Don't bother her.

LOLA.   Mama, give me some tortillas? *(MRS. GARCÍA holds*

out a plate of tortillas. LOLA *puts them in a paper bag.)*

JUANITA.   You can't take tortillas, Lola. The kids laugh at them.

LOLA.   We have to bring a lunch.

CARLOS.   Why doesn't Pancho have to go?

SALVADOR.   Pancho should be going. Papa let him drop out . . .

PANCHO *(rising, swings at* CARLOS, *who ducks).*   Mind your own business.

   *(*MR. GARCÍA *enters from right, pantomimes closing a door behind him.)*

MR. GARCÍA.   Everybody has to work today.

LOLA.   Papa, you said if we worked last week we could go back to school today.

MR. GARCÍA.   The grapes are finished—but Harrison needs extra hands to pick his bean crop. And I must have money for the last payment on my truck.

LOLA.   I was trying to make some friends at school, Papa. They don't like me because I'm absent so much. And I'm two years behind my grade. If I miss any more I won't be promoted *this* year.

MR. GARCÍA.   You're thirteen. You have gone to school as long as anyone in our family.

SALVADOR *(rising, angrily).*   Yes, you made me quit, Papa, and Pancho has dropped out. Now it's Lola?

MR. GARCÍA *(sighing).*   It is not my wish . . .

SALVADOR.   Lola is very smart. You shouldn't make it so hard for her.

MR. GARCÍA.   What can I do? We can't eat school books for dinner.

SALVADOR.   We could earn more money if we had more education. La Causa has taught us this.

MR. GARCÍA.   La Causa—what has this union ever done for us?

SALVADOR.   La Causa is more than a union. It's a great movement of the people. Cesar Chavez is our leader. He is going to make the growers pay us better wages. That's only a start.

MR. GARCÍA *(smiling)*.   Could you please tell this to Harrison—that maybe he should pay us some more?

SALVADOR.   We are telling him, Papa. He'll have to do it before long. But you shouldn't work for Harrison. We're striking against him. He sprays his fields with deadly poisons.

(LOLA *quietly picks up her school books from a chair, waits for her chance, slips out when* MR. GARCÍA *is not looking.* SALVADOR *winks at her. The other children wait, smiling.)*

MR. GARCÍA.   What about the bugs? Should he let them eat the crops before we can pick them?

SALVADOR.   That bug killer also killed my brother.

MR. GARCÍA.   It was an accident. Julio got too close. It's a risk we have to take, in our work.

SALVADOR.   Papa, that spray makes everybody sick—even

people who eat the grapes. Harrison could use a different kind.

MR. GARCÍA *(smiling)*.   Think of it! I have a son who knows more than the man who owns the fields. *(looking around)* Now, where has Lola gone? *(The children are grinning.)* To school? We will have to pick her up on the way. *(He motions to them to come with him.)* Coming, Salvador?

SALVADOR.   Papa, didn't you know the union is picketing Harrison's farm today? I'm going there to help. Want to give me a ride?

> *(MR. GARCÍA takes a swing at him. SALVADOR, laughing, dodges and runs off right.)*

MR. GARCÍA *(shouting after him)*.   Go and march for La Causa!

> *(The Garcías go off right together. The STAGE MANAGER enters carrying a sign that reads "School Playground." LOLA enters from left, followed by SUSAN, GAIL, and RUTH.)*

SUSAN.   Lola, where were you last week?

LOLA.   I had to help my father with the grape pruning.

GAIL.   I bet you don't even know we're having a fiesta.

LOLA.   A fiesta! When?

RUTH.   In about a month. Carmelita is going to teach us a Mexican dance.

LOLA.   Who's Carmelita?

RUTH.   Don't you know? She came from the high school to help Miss Marvin.

GAIL. She's learning to be a teacher.

(ALBERTO *and* MIGUEL, *Mexican Americans, enter from left.*)

RUTH. Lola, you miss so much. Why do you stay out all the time?

LOLA *(hurt)*. I'm working to help my father buy a truck.

GAIL. What do you want with a truck?

MIGUEL. To take them to work in your father's fields.

ALBERTO. And to move in, when they go to another town.

SUSAN. Why are you always moving?

MIGUEL. Because we're migrant workers—we *campesinos* go where the crops are.

(DON *and* FRED, *Anglo-Americans, come on from left.*)

ALBERTO. Somebody has to pick those grapes and apples and tomatoes you like to eat.

FRED. When do you work, then? You Chicanos are always striking and picketing.

ALBERTO. We don't get paid enough to live on. We're striking for better wages.

MIGUEL. And to stop the poison spray.

LOLA. The pesticide. It kills people. It killed my brother.

MIGUEL. It could kill you. Eat those grapes, you're eating poison.

FRED. That's a lie. Why would growers poison their own grapes?

MIGUEL. Because they're *stupid*.

ALBERTO. We're going to picket until we make somebody listen.

MIGUEL. And they better stop hurting our pickets.

GAIL. Who's hurting them?

MIGUEL. Mr. Harrison is your father, no? One of his trucks ran down a man who was picketing.

GAIL. I don't believe it. My father would never allow that.

DON. It's a lie. You Chicanos tell lies. It was an accident.

ALBERTO. You Anglos tell lies. It was not an accident— that driver aimed at Rinaldo. He's in the hospital now, all crippled.

MIGUEL. Yeah, Anglos did that. Anglos! Anglos!

DON. Chicanos! Chicanos!

(The boys begin to tussle, yelling at each other. The girls yell on the sidelines. CARMELITA, a pretty Mexican American high school girl, comes on from left carrying a tambourine. She stops the fight.)

CARMELITA. Here—stop fighting. What's the matter, any-way?

MIGUEL *(struggling to get away from her grasp)*. Those dirty Anglos. They called us Chicanos . . .

FRED *(trying to hit him again)*. Yeah, yeah—Chicanos . . .

CARMELITA. "Chicano" is only a name for Mexican American—just as "Anglo" means English American. I'm proud that I am Chicano. At school we learn to get along with one another—right?

ALBERTO (*sullenly*). We can't get along with Anglos.

CARMELITA. I've seen you play and have good times together. Today we're going to learn a Mexican dance. (*She smiles.*) A Chicano dance. (*shakes the tambourine*) And dancing makes everybody happy.

FRED. Why can't we learn an American dance?

CARMELITA. It is American. America has people from all over the world, who brought their dances with them. Now, let's begin. Take partners. Every Chicano dance with an Anglo! (*The Chicanos stay together.* MIGUEL *chooses* LOLA.) No? Then dance away your anger today. For the fiesta I'll stir you all together—like re-fried beans! (*They laugh.*)

CARMELITA (*continuing, shakes the tambourine*). Here's the first part. (*She steps it off for them, they follow her.*) Good—that's very good. Now, the second part. (*She starts, stops.*) No, I'm doing that wrong. Let's see, one, two, one, two. (*She looks at* LOLA, *who is quietly doing the step.*) Here's somebody who knows it.

MIGUEL. It's Lola. She knows many Chicano dances.

CARMELITA. Come, Lola, show us the step.

GAIL. That's not fair—she's absent all the time.

CARMELITA. She's here today, isn't she? Come, Lola.

LOLA *(drawing away)*. Oh, no—I couldn't—my—my shoes don't fit . . .

CARMELITA. Try, anyway! *(She brings* LOLA *and* MIGUEL *into the center.)* Now, everybody watch. One, two, one, two. (LOLA *finishes the middle part, they follow her lead.* MISS MARVIN, *the teacher, enters in time to see them.* CARMELITA *claps at the end.)* Very good! Wasn't that good, Miss Marvin?

MISS MARVIN. Yes. I didn't know Lola could dance so well. *(*LOLA *is smiling happily.)*

CARMELITA *(hugging* LOLA*)*. Lola, you're going to help us with the fiesta.

LOLA *(joyfully)*. I have a Mexican doll—and a tambourine. Should I bring them?

CARMELITA. Of course. Now, the last part is the first repeated. One, two, one, two.

(She shakes her tambourine, they begin again. MR. GARCÍA *appears at left.* LOLA *stops still. The dance stops.)*

MR. GARCÍA *(to* MISS MARVIN*)*. I have come for my daughter, Lola García. They have called for extra hands today to pick the beans. Her brothers and sisters are waiting in the truck.

MISS MARVIN. Mr. García, Lola has just missed a whole week.

MR. GARCÍA. I am sorry, ma'am. We don't have regular work and pay like you. We have to eat.

MISS MARVIN. Perhaps I could see about some food for your family.

MR. GARCÍA *(proudly)*. No, thank you, we will not accept. We work for our food.

MISS MARVIN. Lola can't be promoted if she misses any more school. Her class will be in junior high next year. Wouldn't you like to get a high school diploma, Lola?

LOLA *(longingly)*. Think of it!

MR. GARCÍA. She is already too far behind.

MISS MARVIN. Lola can graduate. She is a very bright girl. And the law says she must stay in school until she is sixteen.

MR. GARCÍA. That is not enforced very much. Many children stop before that age.

MISS MARVIN. But I believe in this law, Mr. García. It's for Lola's good. If you take her away, I'll have to report it.

MR. GARCÍA *(eyes flashing)*. And if you interfere with my family, I will take them away from this town.

LOLA. Oh, no, Papa!

MR. GARCÍA. The work here is coming to an end. We will just leave a little sooner than I said.

LOLA *(sadly)*. Papa, I might as well quit for good.

MR. GARCÍA. That is so. Come, they are waiting for us.

(MR. GARCÍA walks off right. LOLA looks at her teacher, sighs, follows him. MISS MARVIN, CARMELITA, and the children go off left. The STAGE MANAGER enters right carrying a sign that reads "Harrison Farm." Music

warning of danger plays softly through the pantomime that follows. All the Garcías enter from right. A FORE-MAN *enters left, carrying cardboard cartons.)*

FOREMAN *(handing a carton to each).* Everybody take a row of beans, and start picking. Now, they're spraying the fields today. When the spray rig comes by, be sure you duck down under the plants.

(The Garcías spread out across the stage, each choosing a row. LOLA *works up and down at right. They stoop, pantomime picking beans. Some work on their knees. They begin to fill their cartons.* SALVADOR *and another picket slowly walk from left to right, downstage, back again, off, carrying signs that read "Growers Use Deadly Poison Sprays" and "Workers Strike for Higher Wages." There is the sound of a tractor off right. The* FOREMAN *goes off to meet it.)*

CARLOS *(looking off right).* Look out! Here comes the spray rig.

PANCHO. He's coming right past us. Look out, Lola! He's going to hit your row.

*(*LOLA *pays no attention, goes on picking. The others duck, dodge the oncoming tractor, pantomime watching it go past.* LOLA *chokes, begins to cough, falls and lies still.* MRS. GARCÍA *and* JUANITA *rush to* LOLA.)

MRS. GARCÍA. Lola! Are you all right? Lola, try to get up.

JUANITA. Lola, why didn't you get out of the way? Did you want the spray to hit you?

(They help LOLA *downstage right. She is coughing and*

staggering. The STAGE MANAGER *enters, carrying a sign that reads "García Home." They move upstage right, pantomime opening the door, put* LOLA *on the cot.* SALVADOR *enters, goes to* LOLA *and kneels beside her.* MRS. GARCÍA *stands on the other side. The others tip-toe off right, sit outside the house, waiting anxiously. Lights dim, soft music is heard for a moment, then lights brighten.* LOLA *sits up.)*

MRS. GARCÍA. Thank God my little one is better. Why did you make yourself sick, Lola? (LOLA *shakes her head, puzzled.)*

SALVADOR. I think it was so that Papa couldn't make her leave. But, Lola, if you're sick, you can't go to school, either—and when you get well, Papa can still move.

MRS. GARCÍA. Besides, you could have died.

LOLA. Mama—I'm sorry.

SALVADOR. Be glad you're alive.

(The school children, MISS MARVIN, *and* CARMELITA *cross downstage from left, walk up to the* GARCÍA *door up right, pantomime knocking.* MRS. GARCÍA *goes to the door, lets them in. The García children wait outside.* GAIL *is carrying flowers.* MISS MARVIN *and* GAIL *approach the bed.)*

MISS MARVIN. Lola, we've missed you at school. And we've been so worried. Gail has some flowers for you. (GAIL *hands the flowers to* LOLA.*)*

LOLA *(smiling, amazed).* Thank you, Gail, they're beautiful. Oh, Miss Marvin, how will I ever get caught up?

RUTH.   We're going to help you with your lessons, Lola.

SUSAN.   And we're waiting to have the fiesta when you get well.

GAIL.   Lola, I talked to my father about that terrible spray. I begged him to get a new kind that doesn't hurt people.

SALVADOR.   Good. We've been talking to him, too.

LOLA.   I'm so glad to see everybody.

MISS MARVIN.   Hurry and get well, Lola. We need you to help with our Mexican dance.

(LOLA nods and smiles. MISS MARVIN and the children go out right, CARMELITA stays to visit with LOLA. As they come downstage and walk across left, the García children run after them, calling to them.)

JOSEFINA.   Teacher, is Lola going to dance in the fiesta?

MISS MARVIN *(turning)*.   Lola is going to lead the dance. You're all invited.

(They cheer. MISS MARVIN and the school children go off left. MRS. GARCÍA comes to the door, calls.)

MRS. GARCÍA.   Come, children, we are going to the store now. Lola needs milk for supper. *(The García children follow her off right.)*

CARMELITA *(to SALVADOR)*.   Aren't you Salvador? *(He nods.)*

SALVADOR.   I remember you, Carmelita. We were once in school together. Well, you have all made my sister happy today.

LOLA. To think they came here, to see me, in this awful old house!

CARMELITA. They want to be your friends, Lola. *(LOLA begins to cry.)* Why are you crying?

LOLA. Because I have to go away and leave my friends.

CARMELITA. It's hard, moving from one school to another. I know, because I had to do it, too.

LOLA. How did you ever get promoted?

CARMELITA. I took my school records with me to every town, and asked my teacher to write to the next teacher.

SALVADOR. Think of it, Lola. Someday you'll have a good job and earn much money. And the more you learn, the more you can do for La Causa.

CARMELITA. You should go back to school, Salvador.

SALVADOR. One of these days I will.

LOLA. Couldn't I come and stay with you, Carmelita, when Papa goes?

CARMELITA *(smiling)*. But where would I put another little sister? There are two more sleeping in my bed now. *(She hugs LOLA.)* Come back to school as soon as you can, Lola.

SALVADOR *(to CARMELITA)*. I'll give you a ride home in our new truck. *(They go out together, walk across down left and off. MR. GARCÍA comes to the door, enters, smiling, carrying a package.)*

LOLA. What's in the package, Papa?

MR. GARCÍA.   You have to get well, now, to use these!

(MR. GARCÍA *takes out a new pair of shoes, hands them to* LOLA, *beaming with pride.* MRS. GARCÍA *and the children return, crowd eagerly around.*)

JUANITA.   New shoes!

LOLA.   Oh, they're beautiful, Papa! The nicest I ever had.

PANCHO.   Are they for the fiesta?

LOLA *(putting on the shoes, rises, dances a few steps).* They are for school—and the fiesta. Papa, you bought me shoes for school. You do want me to go!

JUANITA.   But aren't we leaving here?

MR. GARCÍA *(annoyed).*   Are there no schools in the other towns where we work?

LOLA *(hesitates a moment, then makes up her mind).*   Of course, Papa.

MR. GARCÍA.   The work in this county is finished now until August. Lola has to eat good food to get strong. *(to* JUANITA*)* You want a new dress, eh? And one for Josefina, and Elena . . .

MRS. GARCÍA.   And shirts for Carlos and Pancho . . .

ELENA.   And Salvador?

MR. GARCÍA.   La Causa takes care of Salvador!

LOLA.   We must all help Papa now. We'll take our school records with us, so we can be promoted in June.

JUANITA.   But, Lola, you wanted to go to the junior high.

LOLA. Maybe I'll get back. Now everybody must study hard and work for La Causa!

(MR. GARCÍA frowns, shrugs, finally smiles. Dance music comes in; the children rush around getting ready. MRS. GARCÍA gives the boys clean shirts. They put them on. The girls comb their hair, fighting over a small mirror. LOLA puts one of GAIL's flowers in her hair, covers her blouse with a colorful shawl, takes a Mexican doll and a tambourine from the box under the bed. ELENA takes the tambourine, JOSEFINA the doll. MIGUEL and AL-BERTO come to the door at right, call in.)

MIGUEL. Lola, today is the fiesta.

LOLA *(calling out)*. I know—we're getting ready.

(LOLA and the Garcías hurry out of the door, right. The STAGE MANAGER enters carrying a sign that reads "Fiesta, Everyone Invited," puts down the sign, stays. MISS MARVIN, CARMELITA, and the school children enter from left, bringing festoons, quickly decorate the stage. LOLA and FRED lead off in the dance, the rest form couples. The Garcías group down right, clap their hands in time. When the dance comes back to repeat the first part, MISS MARVIN motions to all the Garcías to join in. MR. and MRS. GARCÍA know every step. The dance ends with applause and cheers. LOLA and her family start off right.)

GAIL. Come back next year, Lola. Come to junior high.

MISS MARVIN. Lola, I'm recommending you for promotion in June.

CARMELITA. Write to us, Lola. We'll write to you.

LOLA *(wiping away tears).* Oh, I'll write. I hope I'll see you all next year.

(The Garcías leave to a chorus of good-byes.)

Playing time: 15 minutes.

PRODUCTION NOTES

With the help of the stage manager's signs, the audience can follow the change of scenes from Lola's house to the school yard and the bean field. If you pantomime the door to the house, being careful to walk as if along an outside wall, the audience will believe this, too.

There are many simple Mexican dances that can be used. You will find directions for them in books in your school library. A record or tape can be played offstage for the music. A sound-effects record will have tractor or automobile sounds, or you can use a child's windup toy or a party noisemaker offstage. If you do not have a folding cot in your school, make Lola's bed with chairs and pillows. Costumes can be the clothes you wear. Use bright colors for blouses and shirts and full skirts for the girls. If you want a larger cast, add girls and boys as school children, bean pickers, pickets, or dancers.

GET ON BOARD,
LITTLE CHILDREN

For hundreds of years, European and Middle East traders bought and captured black people in Africa to sell them as slaves. In 1619, they began to bring them to the American colonies for work in the fields—mainly in the South, since most Africans were used to a warm climate.

In the North, slavery did not prove profitable. There were smaller and fewer farms, and the weather was colder. There were more cities where free immigrants worked in factories. By 1860, most of the Northern states had passed laws against slavery. But in the South, the planters depended more and more on slaves to raise and pick cotton. Each year, southern planters sold their crops to be sent north and made into goods that were shipped all over the world. As the cotton industry grew, the number of slaves increased to four million.

Even then, many white Americans in the North and in the South felt that slavery was sinful. They were always talking and thinking of ways to gradually free the slaves. But money was in the picture, too. If a planter paid from $300 to $900 for a slave, he expected a lifetime of free labor from this man or woman. And fortunes were being made in the business of cotton.

A slave had no rights. His marriage was not legal, and his wife and children were often sold to people many miles away. He might never see or hear from them again.

It was against the law for a slave to leave his plantation without a written pass. Slaves who ran away, if caught, were brought back in chains, branded on their faces with the letter "R," and beaten. People who helped them could be fined or imprisoned.

Some slaves lived with masters who treated them kindly. Other slaves were forced to work in the fields from dawn until dark, driven by an overseer's whip. The money earned went into the pockets of their owners.

There were free black men who had worked and saved money and bought themselves from their masters. Others were freed by owners who hated slavery or wanted to reward a faithful slave. Runaways escaped to free states and found jobs, and then helped others to escape. Religious groups, such as the Quakers, began to help.

A movement began around 1800, pressing for laws to abolish, or do away with, slavery. The abolitionists knew it would take years. Meanwhile, they helped runaways to reach the northern free states or Canada, where they could live safely as free men and women. A secret network of people and places was formed to help escaping slaves on their journey. It was called the Underground Railroad. Over the years, it brought 75,000 slaves to freedom. But no way was found to free all slaves until 1865, after the United States had almost destroyed herself in a savage civil war.

People of all races today are still trying to learn to live together in peace. Understanding the struggle of the blacks for freedom in America can help to show us the way.

GET ON BOARD, LITTLE CHILDREN is a kind of history on stage of real happenings in the years of slavery. Most of the characters are people who lived and were leaders then. Wherever it is possible, they speak the same words they spoke at meetings and wrote in their diaries and other books. Such books are documents. That is why this is called a documentary play.

CHARACTERS

(Actors can play more than one part if your cast is small.)

FREDERICK DOUGLASS	SAM
RUNAWAY	MAU-MAU-BETTS
JOHNSON	SOJOURNER TRUTH
MILLER	MRS. GEDNEY
WHITE CHILD	QUAKER GENTLEMAN
ELIJAH LOVEJOY	PETER
CARTARET	QUAKER LADY
WILLIAM LLOYD GARRISON	FATHER
MRS. REYNOLDS	MOTHER
BLACK CHILD	JIM
MRS. CHESTNUT	SUSIE
HARRIET TUBMAN	MRS. AULD
LEVI COFFIN	MR. AULD
UNCLE FRANK	MR. COVEY
HENRY STEVENS	BILL
MRS. COFFIN	

CONDUCTORS, SLAVES, SLAVEOWNERS, ABOLITIONISTS, TOWNSPEOPLE, CHORUS

(Voices are heard singing in a bright, fast tempo.)

CHORUS. The gospel train is a-comin',
      I hear it just at hand,
      I hear the car wheels rumbling
      And rolling through the land.
      Then get on board,
      Little children, get on board,
      Little children, get on board,
      Little children—there's room for many a more.

(Light comes up on a bare stage that may have a back-drop where symbols of black history are painted. The CHORUS *can be onstage at the back, or offstage. Characters bring on the props needed for each scene.* FRED-ERICK DOUGLASS, *a tall, dignified black man, walks down center, speaks to the audience.)*

DOUGLASS.   My name is Frederick Douglass. I was born a slave on Tuckahoe Plantation, on the eastern shore of Maryland. I figure the year was about 1817. *(The baying of hounds is heard. A black man runs on from up right, ragged, breathless, looking everywhere.)* See this man? He's a slave, too, trying to escape to freedom. *(He steps to right side of stage, and stays there except when he enters a scene.)*

RUNAWAY.   Help me, man. Sweet Jesus says to help me.

DOUGLASS.   Where are you going?

RUNAWAY.   North—always north. Traveling at night—following the North Star. Which way is the river?

DOUGLASS *(pointing off left)*.   That way, about two more miles.

RUNAWAY.   Been beaten twice for running away, till my back's like raw meat. They catch me this time, they'll beat me to death. Master done told me. How'm I going to get across that river?

DOUGLASS.   There's a boat—sometimes you've got to swim it. Friends are on the other side to help you. Ohio is a free state.

RUNAWAY.   A free state! Man, I'm on my way. Pray I'll make it.

DOUGLASS.   Here's another slave who ran away to freedom. Her name is Harriet Tubman.

(HARRIET TUBMAN, *a small black woman, enters right, singing "Go Down, Moses." The* CHORUS *sings every other line.*)

HARRIET *and* CHORUS.   When Israel was in Egypt Land
                (Let my people go)
                Oppressed so hard they could not
                  stand
                (Let my people go).
                Go down, Moses,
                Way down in Egypt land,
                Tell old Pharaoh
                Let my people go.

DOUGLASS.   That was Harriet's favorite song.

HARRIET.   The white people were afraid of that song— might stir up the darkies, they said. *(She chuckles.)*

DOUGLASS.   Moses and the Israelites—weren't they slaves, too, in Egypt?

HARRIET.   Yes—I'm singing about slaves in this country.

DOUGLASS.   Slaves were running away, right from the start. We had a grapevine telegraph going. See? People were passing the word along the grapevine, all about how to escape.

(*During this speech, black men and women run onstage from left and right, meet, form a chain, pantomime a grapevine, passing messages, whispering to the next*

one, right to left. Then, one by one, they run offstage
left until all are gone.)

BLACK CHILD *(from the audience).* I'd like to ask you
something.

WHITE CHILD *(from the audience).* Me, too.

DOUGLASS. Come up here so we can talk.

(The two run up to meet DOUGLASS *downstage right.
They stay there to watch the rest of the play.)*

BLACK CHILD. I want to know how *my* people got to be
slaves to *his* people. *(He swings at* WHITE CHILD, *teasing.)*

WHITE CHILD *(laughing, pushes* BLACK CHILD *away).*
Wasn't *my* idea.

BLACK CHILD *(wrestling with* WHITE CHILD *).* Better not be!

WHITE CHILD. You're all hung up on that.

DOUGLASS *(separating them).* I'll show you how it came
about—and why he's so "hung up," as you call it.

BLACK CHILD. How did slavery get started in this country?

DOUGLASS. There was big money to be made on human
beings. In 1619, slave traders were capturing black people
in Africa. They started bringing them here to sell to white
farmers—for $200, $500, $1000, or more.

MRS. REYNOLDS *(entering right).* You must remember
slaves are ignorant savages. You can't treat them like white
people.

LOVEJOY *(entering left).* They are human beings. You
cannot regard them as your property.

MRS. CHESTNUT *(entering right)*.   Slavery has to go, and joy go with it. I hate it.

GARRISON *(entering left)*.   Let there be but one slave on the face of the globe—I must defend his rights.

MRS. REYNOLDS *(with folded hands)*.   It is true they are slaves, but their chains never clank. Each link is kept moist and bright with the oil of kindness. It is the will of God.

(LOVEJOY, MRS. REYNOLDS, MRS. CHESTNUT, and GARRISON go off as they came.)

DOUGLASS.   Is *this* the will of God?

(Slaves and white buyers come onstage and pantomime the sale of slaves on an auction block. A slave with hands tied mounts the block. Buyers gather around to bid. CHORUS sings softly, first two lines of "Nobody Knows the Trouble I've Seen.")

CHORUS *(singing)*. Nobody knows the trouble I've seen,
                     Nobody knows but Jesus.

DOUGLASS.   That's a slave auction—people being sold to the man who offers the most money.

CHORUS *(sings)*. Nobody knows the trouble I've seen—
                   Glory, Hallelujah!
                   Sometimes I'm up, sometimes I'm down,
                   Oh, yes, Lord,
                   Sometimes I'm almost to the ground,
                   Oh, yes, Lord.
                   (Repeat the first four lines.)

(During the singing the pantomime continues. An auctioneer gestures as if describing the slave's strength,

uses his gavel, people raise their hands, bidding. One man outbids the rest, walks away, leading the slave by a rope.)

DOUGLASS. That was permitted by law throughout the South and sometimes in the North.

BLACK CHILD *(as the slave is led away)*. Look at that. Couldn't somebody stop 'em?

DOUGLASS. A lot of people were trying—that's what abolition was all about.

(The CHORUS continues singing softly. Pantomime shows two children being sold away from their mother. She tries to hold them but is jerked roughly back by two white men.)

WHITE CHILD. Hey, they can't do that—those kids don't want to leave their mother!

DOUGLASS. And their mother would rather die than let them go.

WHITE CHILD *(calling to the two men as they lead the children off)*. You come back here—you bring those children back. *(He starts to run after them. One of the men turns, comes down right to talk to him. The other man continues off left with the children.)*

WHITE MAN *(to WHITE CHILD)*. I'm really sorry. I wanted to buy the mother, too, but the bidding went too high.

WHITE CHILD. Then you didn't have to buy the children.

WHITE MAN *(shaking his head)*. It happens every day—there's nothing I can do. I'm always good to my slaves.

(WHITE MAN *goes off left with* BUYERS, AUCTIONEERS, *and* SLAVES.)

DOUGLASS. The law said a slave was nothing but a piece of property. The only way out was to help these folks escape. That's how the Underground Railroad started.

WHITE CHILD. Why was this railroad called "Underground"?

DOUGLASS. Because it was all kept secret. It was a way a slave could travel without getting caught, from the deep South to Canada. Free black men and friendly whites helped him to hide. Even in free states, rewards were offered for catching a runaway slave. And if you helped a slave to escape, you could be sent to prison.

WHITE CHILD. Were there real trains, on a real track?

DOUGLASS. No, the track might be a path through the woods or a boat crossing the river—always heading north.

BLACK CHILD. How did they find it?

DOUGLASS. Slaves made plans with somebody on the outside. They might wait for months, until word came to start—a letter or a message on the grapevine, sometimes a song.

(CHORUS *sings "Swing Low, Sweet Chariot."* MRS. REYNOLDS *enters from right, stands listening.*)

CHORUS. Swing low, sweet chariot,
    Coming for to carry me home,
    Swing low, sweet chariot,
    Coming for to carry me home.
    I looked over Jordan, and what did I see,

Coming for to carry me home,
A band of angels, coming after me,
Coming for to carry me home.
(Repeat first four lines.)

MRS. REYNOLDS.   Slaves are simple people. They sing at their work and in the evenings. Listen to that—don't they sound happy? *(She pauses a moment as the* CHORUS *softly hums another line or two; then she goes out right.)*

DOUGLASS.   Mrs. Reynolds never guessed the truth—that song was a signal. If you heard "Swing Low, Sweet Chariot" under your cabin window in the night, what would you think it meant? *(*BLACK CHILD *and* WHITE CHILD *think hard.)* Think about the words. What would a chariot mean?

WHITE CHILD.   A chariot—Oh, I get it! A seat on the underground train!

BLACK CHILD.   "Coming for to carry me home"—that means it's time to start!

DOUGLASS.   You're right. Maybe in a wagon, hiding under a load of straw.

(Black people walk on from right to left, whispering, fingers on their lips, listening. A hoot-owl call is heard: "T-woo, t-woo, t-woo.")

DOUGLASS.   Hear the owl hooting three times? That's a signal the conductors used.

BLACK CHILD.   That railroad had conductors?

DOUGLASS.   There are some conductors, passing the fugitives along.

72

(CONDUCTORS enter, place themselves across the stage. They are in Quaker dress. They whisper information from one to the next, right to left. The FUGITIVES group down right, one moves along the line. Each CONDUCTOR takes the FUGITIVE's hand encouragingly, passes him left, to the next CONDUCTOR. CONDUCTORS speak in rhythm, saying their lines faster and faster until it begins to sound like a locomotive.)

FIRST CONDUCTOR.   Go to the river.

(The FUGITIVE moves to the SECOND CONDUCTOR.)

SECOND CONDUCTOR *(passing the FUGITIVE left)*.   Wait for a boat.

THIRD CONDUCTOR *(passing FUGITIVE left)*.   Friends will meet you . . .

FOURTH CONDUCTOR *(passing FUGITIVE left as he goes off-stage)*. With food and clothes.

(This is repeated with a second FUGITIVE. Then the FUGITIVES begin to come by faster. The four CONDUCTORS close ranks, each moving his arm in a circle like the turning of locomotive wheels as they chant the lines together.)

CONDUCTORS *(all together)*.   Go to the river—wait for a boat—friends will meet you with food and clothes.

(The pantomime and lines continue, faster and faster. CONDUCTORS move left with FUGITIVES, and all go off-stage left.)

DOUGLASS.   The chariot had to have a locomotive . . .

WHITE CHILD.   Horses! Horses drawing the wagons—they

were the locomotives!

BLACK CHILD. The wagons were the cars on the train!

DOUGLASS. And every railroad has to have stations along the way.

WHITE CHILD. Stations were the houses where conductors took the passengers to hide.

DOUGLASS. You're catching on. And the man who owned the house was the stationmaster.

BLACK CHILD. That's right—they needed a stationmaster!

(LEVI COFFIN *enters from left, dressed as a Quaker.*)

DOUGLASS. Levi Coffin was a stationmaster for many years. Will you tell these children what they called you, Mr. Coffin?

COFFIN *(proudly).* They called me the president of the Underground Railroad.

DOUGLASS. When did you start helping runaways?

COFFIN. When I was a boy in North Carolina, I started a school to teach slaves to read the Bible. Everybody liked the idea, and the slaves were allowed to come on Sunday afternoon.

(COFFIN *arranges a few stools for his school. Several* SLAVES *enter, sit.* COFFIN *opens a Bible. An old black preacher,* UNCLE FRANK, *kneels in prayer.* COFFIN *and the others kneel.*)

UNCLE FRANK. Oh, Lord, put it in our hearts to learn to read the good book. Make the letters big and plain, and make our eyes bright and shining.

SLAVES. Yes, Lord!

That's right. *(All speak at once, so that it*

Amen. *sounds like a crowd.)*

UNCLE FRANK. Make our minds sharp as a double-edged sword, so we can see clean through the book.

SLAVES. Amen.

UNCLE FRANK. Teach us to be good servants, and touch our masters' hearts and make 'em tender, so they will not lay the whips to our bare backs anymore.

SLAVES. No!

No more. *(All speak at once.)*

UNCLE FRANK. And you, great Master, shall have all the glory.

SLAVES. Amen. Praise the Lord. *(They rise and sit on the stools.)*

COFFIN *(standing)*. Uncle Frank, will thee read us from the Bible? *(He hands the open book to* UNCLE FRANK.*)*

UNCLE FRANK *(reading with difficulty)*. You—shall—know—the truth—and the truth—shall make you—free!

SLAVES. Amen.

Yes, Lord. *(All speak at once.)*

That's right.

(Two white men break in on the scene.)

FIRST MAN. Coffin, you've got to close this school.

UNCLE FRANK *(rising)*. Why, Master? Why you want to

do that? Our masters all say we could come.

SECOND MAN.   'Most everybody in the county is against it now.

COFFIN.   Against learning to read the Bible?

FIRST MAN.   It's stirring up the other slaves.

SECOND MAN.   You'll have to give it up.

   *(*WHITE MEN *herd* COFFIN *and* SLAVES *off right.* SLAVES *are silent and sad.)*

COFFIN *(calling angrily as he follows).*   Thee cannot stifle knowledge . . .

DOUGLASS.   Coffin was right and so were those men Knowledge makes a man unfit to be a slave.

BLACK CHILD.   What happened to Levi Coffin?

DOUGLASS.   He moved to Newport, Indiana, a town on the underground line. Quakers and free blacks were there, helping slaves escape.

   *(*COFFIN *and* HENRY STEVENS, *a Quaker, enter.)*

COFFIN.   Those slave catchers that were hanging around here just captured two fugitives, Henry.

STEVENS.   The colored people here do their best to hide runaways.

COFFIN.   Why don't we Quakers hide them in our homes?

STEVENS.   Levi, the law is very severe against aiding runaway slaves. And this is dangerous, too. Slaves sometimes kill their masters in their frenzy to get away. Must we hide murderers in our homes, and give them the chance to murder us?

COFFIN.   Did the Good Samaritan stop to ask if that man in trouble was a criminal?

STEVENS *(laughing).*   Thee has put me to shame with thy courage, Levi Coffin. We will pass the word along.

(STEVENS puts an arm around COFFIN. They go off left.)

DOUGLASS.   Levi's house became an important station on the Underground Railroad. Let's watch this. A fugitive is arriving about 2 A.M. Levi and his wife are always on call.

(Four men enter silently from right, carrying a large heavy packing box. One, dressed as a Quaker, pantomimes knocking on door at left.)

COFFIN *(calling from offstage).*   Who's there?

FIRST CONDUCTOR.   A friend with friends.

DOUGLASS.   That was the password of the Quakers—they're also called the Religious Society of Friends.

(COFFIN enters, pantomimes opening the door, looks at the box.)

COFFIN.   Something in that box for me?

SECOND CONDUCTOR.   Yes, Mr. Coffin. It's perishable, too.

(FIRST CONDUCTOR pries up boards with a crowbar. They pull them off, look inside.)

FIRST CONDUCTOR.   Give me a hand, now.

(They carefully lift a black man out of the box. He is weak and frightened, looks around nervously.)

SECOND CONDUCTOR. There you are, Sam.

(MRS. COFFIN enters carrying a glass of water, offers it to SAM. He drinks thirstily.)

MRS. COFFIN. Easy, now—not too fast. *(to DOUGLASS)* They're always famished for water.

FIRST CONDUCTOR. Better get him inside. We shook off two slave catchers at the state line.

COFFIN. He'll be hungry, too.

SAM. Yes, sir—starved.

COFFIN. Thee will have a treat when thee tastes my wife's cooking.

MRS. COFFIN. We'll see that he gets some rest, too. To-morrow night, Levi will get him started to the next station.

(They help him off into the house. CONDUCTORS hurry away.)

DOUGLASS *(pointing offstage right)*. Look there—not a bit too soon, either.

(JOHNSON and MILLER enter right, hurry to COFFIN's door, knock. COFFIN waits as long as he can before answering.)

COFFIN *(calling sleepily from offstage)*. Who is it?

JOHNSON. Mr. Coffin, have you seen any fugitive slaves around here?

COFFIN *(enters left, wearing a nightcap)*. What does thee mean by slaves? In the eyes of God, all men are free.

MILLER *(impatiently)*. Now, Mr. Coffin, you know what we mean. Aren't you hiding a fugitive here tonight?

JONES.   It's well known that you help runaway slaves.

COFFIN.   I did not know I was so famous.

WILLIAMS.   Are you going to let us in or aren't you?

COFFIN.   The law requires thee to have a writ to search my premises.

JOHNSON *(rudely trying to push past)*.   We'll go into that someday in court.

COFFIN *(blocking him)*.   Hold on, young fellow. I could have thee arrested as a kidnapper.

JOHNSON.   A kidnapper!

COFFIN.   If thee should enter my house without a writ and take away any person inside, I can charge thee with kidnapping.

(*The two men stand in angry silence.*)

JOHNSON.   Coffin, *thy* house just may burn down someday.

MILLER.   And *thy* store.

JOHNSON.   Something could happen to *thee,* too.

COFFIN.   A man of peace does not fear threats. And now if thee will excuse me—I'd like to get back to my bed.

(*The men go sullenly off right.* COFFIN *looks at* DOUGLASS.)

COFFIN.   I never lost a one that way. *(He goes off left.)*

BLACK CHILD.   Mr. Douglass, those slaves escaping—they're all in such a hurry. I'd like to see some of 'em longer.

DOUGLASS. You're talking to me—I'm an escaped slave. I'll show you some others.

(CHORUS *sings "My Lord, What a Mourning."*)

CHORUS. My Lord, what a mourning,
My Lord, what a mourning,
My Lord, what a mourning,
When the stars begin to fall!

(*During the singing a tall, thin black woman walks by, meets another black woman at center.*)

DOUGLASS. This is Sojourner Truth. (*pointing to the thin woman*) She was born a slave in New York State. And that's Mau-Mau-Betts, Sojourner's mother. Mau-Mau had a big family, but most of her children were sold away.

MAU-MAU-BETTS (*sadly*). Now your little brother, he's gone. Master found him hiding behind the woodpile.

SOJOURNER. Didn't you pray to the Lord, Mau-Mau? How come he let Master take your children away?

MAU-MAU-BETTS. The good Lord helping all my children, wherever they be. Kneel down and pray with me. (*They kneel.*) Ask God for help. (MAU-MAU *looks up.*) See those stars up there? Remember they shining on all your brothers and sisters, sold away and scattered—the same God loving and helping us all.

CHORUS (*sings softly as they pray*).
You'll hear the trumpet sound
To wake the nations underground,
Looking to my God's right hand
When the stars begin to fall.
(*Repeat first four lines.*)

(As the song ends, SOJOURNER *rises, comes downstage.* MAU-MAU-BETTS *goes off.)*

SOJOURNER. The New York law made me free in 1827, and it said my son, Peter, couldn't be sold out of the state. But my master sent Peter to Alabama with the Gedney girl. I went to Mrs. Gedney.

*(*MRS. GEDNEY, *a white woman, enters, meets* SO-JOURNER *at center.)*

SOJOURNER. Mrs. Gedney, ma'am—I want my son back. You got to get him back for me. The law says so.

MRS. GEDNEY. What a fuss about nothing. Your son will be treated well and have plenty of everything.

SOJOURNER. But my boy has gone to be a slave. And he's too little to be away from his mother.

MRS. GEDNEY. It's all settled—there's nothing I can do. *(She goes off.)*

SOJOURNER. Then I prayed to the Lord and I went to the Quakers for help. They took the case into court.

(A QUAKER *enters, bringing* PETER, *a little black boy.)*

QUAKER. Here is thy son, Sojourner.

*(*SOJOURNER *joyfully holds out her arms.* PETER *shrinks away, tries to hide behind* QUAKER.*)*

PETER. Don't know—don't know who that is.

QUAKER. He has been beaten and is afraid. *(to* PETER*)* Thee is quite safe with thy mother now.

SOJOURNER. Praise be to God! How did it come to pass?

QUAKER. Gedney was breaking the law. He had to bring

Peter back or face fourteen years in prison. *(to* PETER*)*
Thy mother will care for thee now.

*(*QUAKER *goes off.* PETER *comes shyly to* SOJOURNER, *who holds him beside her for a moment.)*

SOJOURNER.   Your supper's ready, Peter, and you'll sleep in your own bed tonight.

*(*PETER *goes off.)*

SOJOURNER.   Once my old master tried to get me back—and God stood in my path and blocked my way. Then I saw Jesus! He came like a friend, to help me. And I felt such a love in my soul as I never felt before. And the whole world got bright, and the trees, they waved in glory, and every little bit of stone on the ground shone like glass. And I shouted, "Praise, praise, praise to the Lord."

DOUGLASS.   Sojourner Truth—how did you come by that name?

SOJOURNER.   One day the spirit called me to make a journey east, to tell people about Jesus. And on my way I met a Quaker lady.

*(*QUAKER LADY *enters from left.)*

QUAKER LADY.   Good morning.

SOJOURNER.   Good morning, ma'am.

QUAKER LADY.   Thee is out early this morning. What is thy name?

SOJOURNER.   The spirit has given me a new name, ma'am. I call myself Sojourner because I'm always traveling, like a pilgrim.

QUAKER LADY. Thee is a slave?

SOJOURNER. I was born a slave. When I was free, I needed a last name of my own—so I said to God one day, "God, give me a name with a handle to it." And I heard a voice say, "Truth." I said, "Why, thank you, God. That's a good name. You're my master now, and Your name is Truth. Truth shall be my abiding name until I die."

QUAKER LADY *(taking* SOJOURNER's *hand).* God bless thee, Sojourner Truth.

*(*QUAKER LADY *goes off right;* SOJOURNER *goes off left.)*

DOUGLASS. William Lloyd Garrison and Elijah Lovejoy were working right along for freedom. Lovejoy started a newspaper, *The Observer.*

*(*LOVEJOY *enters right, holding a copy of his paper.)*

LOVEJOY *(reading).* The time is soon coming when we must all be tried by fire.

DOUGLASS. But angry mobs attacked Lovejoy and destroyed his printing press.

(A mob rushes out behind LOVEJOY, *overtakes him, forces him off left.)*

DOUGLASS. William Lloyd Garrison was attacked by a mob in Boston.

(The mob returns from left, leading GARRISON *across the stage, his hands bound.)*

FIRST MAN. Mr. Garrison, you are too excited. You are on fire.

GARRISON.   I need to be on fire. I have icebergs around me to melt.

SECOND MAN.   Slavery was consented to by the founders of this country.

FIRST MAN.   The business of this whole nation is based on slavery—millions of dollars involved.

GARRISON.   Yes, the North grows rich on the agony of the South.

SECOND MAN.   We're going to put an end to you abolitionists.

GARRISON.   I have seized the trumpet of God. I cannot choose but to obey His voice. *(They hustle him off right.)*

DOUGLASS.   Garrison had many friends—they helped him get away. But in Alton, Illinois, a free state, the mob finally silenced Lovejoy the only way it could ever be done.

(LOVEJOY enters, men follow, threatening him.)

LOVEJOY.   While I live, I cannot hold my peace.

FIRST MAN.   Get him—get Elijah Lovejoy.

SECOND MAN.   Kill him!

LOVEJOY *(turns, faces them)*.   If I am to die, it cannot be in a better cause.

(A muffled shot is heard; LOVEJOY falls dead. The men run off. An ABOLITIONIST enters, speaks over LOVE-JOY's dead body.)

ABOLITIONIST.   Elijah Lovejoy, the first American martyr to abolition and the freedom of the press. Murdered

November 7, 1837. For the rights of every man, Lovejoy bowed his head in death.

(The men return and carry off LOVEJOY'*s body.)*

DOUGLASS. The slave population grew to four million. And the Underground Railroad got more powerful all the time. Newspapers began to carry ads like these.

*(*CHORUS *sings "Get on Board, Little Children." People cross the stage carrying placards that read: "Liberty Line," "Improved and Splendid Locomotives," "Benefit Your Health by a Northern Tour," "Necessary Clothing Furnished to Those Who Have Fallen Among Thieves."* CHORUS *changes to "Go Down, Moses."* HARRIET TUBMAN *enters from right, dressed as a man.)*

DOUGLASS. Remember Harriet Tubman, the Moses of her people? Harriet escaped from a Maryland plantation about 1849.

HARRIET. I got to Philadelphia and the Quakers hid me, and then they found me a job. I'm saving my money 'cause I'm going back to help my friends get away. *(She goes off left.)*

DOUGLASS. They called her Moses. Word got around fast —Moses might be coming. Sometimes she would pass through in the night and leave a message.

(A black family enters from right. The mother holds a baby. The father pantomimes building a fire.)

FATHER *(stops, stares at hearth).* Moses was here last night.

MOTHER. How you know it was her?

FATHER.   She done left us a map! Looka here.

MOTHER.   You mean those scratchin's on the hearth? Nothing but the children playing.

JIM.   No, ma'am. We ain't been drawing nothing there.

FATHER.   See this line? Here's the river. You cross the river, and you head north. Everybody say, follow the North Star far enough, you be a free man. About a night's journey, there's an underground station, little place called Centerville. All we got to do is get to that station.

JIM.   How we going to do all that?

FATHER.   Waiting for Moses now. She coming to help us this very night.

HARRIET *(singing softly offstage)*.   Let my people go!

*(*JIM *leaps to the door.* FATHER *holds him back, pantomimes cautiously opening it a crack, listens.)*

FATHER.   Who's there?

HARRIET *(offstage)*.   Moses. *(She enters, a man's hat pulled over her face.)* Slip out and don't make no noise. I got paregoric to give the baby so he won't cry.

MOTHER *(embracing her)*.   Moses! You really here?

SUSIE.   Mama, we going tonight? Ain't we got to go to bed at all?

MOTHER *(stopping her mouth)*.   Hush yo' mouth, and pick up yo' things and *tiptoe.*

(They scurry about in great excitement, gathering up belongings, go off silently, left.)

DOUGLASS. Harriet Tubman made nineteen journeys to the South, helping her family, friends, people she didn't know, to escape.

(People walk by carrying placards that read "Wanted, Harriet Tubman, Dead or Alive. Reward Offered." Each placard lists a higher figure, up to $40,000.)

DOUGLASS. Forty thousand dollars—that was a big heap of money then. But Harriet never stopped till she freed over three hundred slaves.

HARRIET *(entering left)*. On my underground railroad, I never ran my train off the track, and I never lost a passenger.

(BLACK CHILD and WHITE CHILD applaud as she goes off.)

DOUGLASS. I told you I was born a slave. For a while I lived with a family in Baltimore. They were kind in many ways. My mistress even tried to teach me to read. *(He moves upstage, sits on a stool.)*

(MRS. AULD enters, sits on another stool, opens a book.)

DOUGLASS *(reading slowly)*. The Lord—is—my—shepherd —I shall not—want . . .

(MR. AULD enters.)

MR. AULD. Fred, bring in some wood for the fire.

(DOUGLASS gets up, goes off left.)

MRS. AULD. Couldn't that wait a little while, Hugh? Fred is doing so well with his reading lesson . . .

MR. AULD. I don't want you to give him any more lessons.

MRS. AULD. But he has such a good mind, it's a pleasure to teach him.

MR. AULD. You must remember Fred is a slave. Learning will spoil the best nigger in the world.

(They go off. DOUGLASS *returns, carrying a copybook.)*

DOUGLASS. Master was too late. Mistress had taught me enough to make me hungry for more. *(to* CHILDREN*)* How would you like it if folks told you you couldn't go to school? Would you miss it?

WHITE CHILD. Not me!

DOUGLASS. Sure about that?

WHITE CHILD. Well, I guess I don't want anybody saying I *can't go.*

BLACK CHILD. No, sir!

DOUGLASS. I learned to write and spell, copying the words over and over, from this old book. *(He turns to the audience.)* I never had a day of school in my life—but I got myself an education.

*(*COVEY, *a white man, and* BILL, *a black man, enter.* COVEY *carries a bull whip.* DOUGLASS *joins them at center.)*

DOUGLASS. After I was grown, they hired me out on plantations. I got whipped like all the other slaves when my work didn't suit the master. One day I just had enough.

COVEY. Fred, you took an hour to hitch that team—and then you wrecked my wagon.

DOUGLASS. Nobody ever showed me how to hitch a team, Master.

(COVEY raises the whip threateningly. DOUGLASS takes hold of it, struggles with him.)

COVEY. Are you going to resist your punishment, you scoundrel?

DOUGLASS. Yes, sir.

COVEY *(to BILL, who is watching).* Take hold of him, Bill.

BILL. I'm here to work, Mr. Covey, not to help you whip Fred.

DOUGLASS. Bill, don't you put your hands on me.

BILL. Fred, I ain't going to touch you.

DOUGLASS. You're not going to touch me any more, either, Mr. Covey. *(He snatches the whip and hurls it offstage. COVEY goes off, raging. BILL follows, smiling happily. DOUGLASS comes downstage.)* Word got around that Frederick was hard to whip, and after that they let me alone. When I was about twenty-one I escaped on the Underground Railroad to New Bedford, Massachusetts. I'll never forget the first money I ever earned as a free man. A lady had a load of coal she wanted put away, so I stacked it for her in the cellar.

(A lady enters. DOUGLASS moves toward her.)

LADY. You did a nice job, Frederick. What will you charge?

DOUGLASS *(amazed).* What will I *charge?* *(He smiles.)* What will I charge! Why, I guess about a dollar, ma'am. *(She hands him two half dollars, goes off. He comes downstage, shows the money to* BLACK CHILD *and* WHITE CHILD.*)* What would I charge! I could name my own price, and no master could take it away. I was holding two silver half dollars in my hand, and I could earn more. The joy! You have to be a slave to know that feeling.

WHITE CHILD. Did you join the abolitionists?

DOUGLASS. Yes, I began to speak at meetings and tell my story. In one town I borrowed a dinner bell and went through the streets.

(He picks up a large bell and starts across the stage, ringing it. People walk by, looking at him curiously.)

DOUGLASS. Notice! Notice! Frederick Douglass, recently a slave, will speak on Grafton Common this evening at seven o'clock.

WOMAN. Are you a slave?

DOUGLASS. I was a slave, ma'am. Now I am as free as you. Come and hear my story tonight.

MAN. Aren't you afraid of being captured?

DOUGLASS. Yes—but I must live like a man, and help to free my brothers. *(He rings the bell.)* Everybody welcome—come to the Common tonight. *(The crowd groups around him. He turns to the audience.)* One night on Nantucket Island I stood on the platform with William Lloyd Garrison and Sojourner Truth. *(*GARRISON *and* SOJOURNER *join him. He addresses the crowd onstage.)* I'm not going to tell my name, or the name of my master. It's dangerous for me. Let's just say I am a thing—a chattel.

WHITE CHILD.   What is a chattel?

DOUGLASS.   If you don't know that, you'd better look it up. You'll find a dictionary out there. *(He points off right.* BLACK CHILD *and* WHITE CHILD *hurry off right.)*

GARRISON.   Are we listening to a thing, a piece of property, or a man?

CROWD.   A man! A man!

GARRISON.   Will you protect him as a brother man?

CROWD.   Yes!
As a brother.   *(All speak at once.)*
A brother man.

SOJOURNER.   Frederick is my brother. I, too, was born a slave, and I bear the marks of the lash.

GARRISON.   Americans, we hear your boasts of liberty, the merry peal of your bells. We also hear the clanking of chains!

(The CHILDREN *return.)*

WHITE CHILD.   A chattel is an article of property . . .

BLACK CHILD.   Like furniture, livestock—a slave!

DOUGLASS.   The law says a slave can be bought and sold like a sack of flour or a side of bacon.

GARRISON.   Help us to free the slaves, my friends, if you expect to be forgiven by God and find salvation in the life to come.

(The crowd cheers. All go offstage except DOUGLASS *and the two* CHILDREN. CHORUS *sings "Walk Together, Children.")*

CHORUS.   Oh, walk together, children
            Don't you get weary.
            Walk together, children,
            Don't you get weary.
            Walk together, children,
            Don't you get weary.
            There's a great camp meeting in the promised
                land.

DOUGLASS.   Good and evil men were locked in the struggle
    for sixty-five years. The terrible war that resulted almost
    destroyed our country. Many slaves died fighting for their
    own freedom. When it was finally over, we were all free.

    (LEVI COFFIN enters.)

COFFIN.   I wish to announce that the Underground Rail-
    road has carried out its purpose. As president, I now de-
    clare it dissolved—in the hands of the receivers.

    *(CHORUS cheers, marches around the stage in triumph,
    sings another verse, "Oh, shout together, children,"
    etc.)*

DOUGLASS.   Ex-slaves had to learn to read and write, hold
    jobs, earn a living. Most of them had never even handled
    any money. The long struggle for equal rights was just
    beginning.

BLACK CHILD.   What did you do after the war, Mr. Doug-
    lass?

DOUGLASS.   I became a writer, a leader of my people, a
    high official in the United States government.

    *(The entire cast gathers on stage during this speech.
    Three men step out, one by one, to speak to DOUGLASS.)*

FIRST MAN. Mr. Douglass, your newspaper, *The North Star,* has reached a circulation of 4,000. *(The crowd applauds, cheers.)*

SECOND MAN. Mr. Douglass, President Lincoln wants to consult with you. *(The crowd cheers louder.)*

THIRD MAN. Mr. Douglass, President Harrison has appointed you Consul General to Haiti. *(The crowd cheers long and happily.)*

DOUGLASS. We still have much to do. As the song says, walk together, children, and don't get weary. To you who have lived to enjoy the fruits of victory, I can say I, too, live and rejoice.

CHORUS *(in a great shout).* Freedom now! Freedom now! *(All begin to sing, "Get on Board, Little Children.")*

DOUGLASS *(to the audience).* Everybody sing!

(The cast forms a procession and marches around the stage, some of the characters grouped as in their scenes, during the singing of several verses. As each group comes down to the edge of the stage, they encourage the audience to sing with them.)

CURTAIN

Playing time: 30 minutes.

This play is performed best with simple staging and a lively tempo. It must not drag. You are giving your audience many facts mixed in with exciting happenings, and it is important to talk to them, let them feel as close to you as possible, and hold their interest all the way. No scenery is needed; in fact, it would get in your way in this kind of play. For the costumes, a few touches to suggest the time of the play are all you need. Try for long, full skirts for the women, wide white collars and dark clothes for the Quakers, and rough, sack-like garments for the slaves. Let Douglass wear a plain dark shirt and trousers, since he must move quickly from the past to the present, as well as from one kind of scene to another. Only a few very simple props are called for in the script, and the actors can handle these.

Music can be created by children singing in the background, or with harmonicas or other simple instruments at times if you want to use them. The singing will sound more real if there is no piano accompaniment. There are sound-effect records with gunshots and the baying of hounds if you want to use one, or you can work out your own "live" sounds backstage and tape them or not, as you choose. Most of the songs are familiar ones that can be found in many collections of Negro spirituals, with all the verses. The one song that may be a little harder to find is "Walk Together, Children." It is included in J. Rosamund Johnson's collection *The Second Book of Negro Spirituals,* page 180. This is published by The Viking Press.

LOOK BEHIND THE MASK

Somebody move out of here?

JOHN.　Yeah. My pop helped move the furniture yesterday.

MARTA.　How come they left that trunk?

JOHN.　It belongs to Mr. Vivo. I guess he's coming back for it.

ALICE.　Who's Mr. Vivo?

JOHN.　He's an actor—or a magician, or something.

ALICE.　A magician! *(She goes over to the trunk.)* Oh, look —it says "Personal Property—do not touch."

MARTA.　Must be something special.

JOHN.　Leave it alone.

MARTA.　He forgot to lock it! *(She raises the lid cautiously, looks inside. The others gather around.)*

ALICE.　Old clothes—no, costumes! Look, here's a crown— and a scepter. *(She holds them up.)*

JOHN.　Leave that stuff alone, I tell you. If we get caught, it'll be my fault.

PETE.　What's the matter, you chicken?

MARTA.　If anybody comes, we can split.

(They begin to pull parts of costumes out of the trunk and walk about, acting the parts.)

MARTA *(putting on a big hat with plumes).*　I'm a famous actress. I'm a star.

ALICE *(putting the crown on her head).*　I'm a queen. I'm

queen of a big country—it stretches far away, for miles. *(She looks out over the audience, hands spread wide. She waves her scepter, walks about the stage.)* You have to bow when I walk by. Bow, everybody! *(The others make sweeping mock bows.)*

PETE *(finds another crown, puts it on).* I'm a king. Man, I'm king of the biggest country there is. *(He snatches the scepter away from* ALICE, *struts about.)* You better bow when *I* walk by.

*(*JOHN *gives in, puts on a jester's cap, follows* PETE *around, mimicking him.)*

ALICE *(rummaging deep inside the trunk, holds up a package).* What's this? *(She reads, hesitating a little over the words.)* "Superpsychic-hypnotic-magnetic properties —not to be opened." *(Startled, she drops it.)* Ouch—I think it shocked me.

JOHN. I told you not to fool with that stuff.

*(*PETE *grabs the package, opens it cautiously.)*

PETE. Does feel kinda funny. *(He takes out a handful of ferocious-looking masks.)* Look at these—masks! They're magic! *(He tosses them to the others, who take them gingerly, putting back their other costumes.* PETE *discards his crown, puts on a dragon mask, begins to roar.)* I'm a dragon. I've got magic powers—I eat little children!

MARTA *(putting on a werewolf mask).* I'm a werewolf— a hungry werewolf. *(She howls eerily.)*

ALICE *(putting on a bat mask).* And I'm a vampire bat— I'll suck your blood. *(She flaps her arms like wings, flits around.)*

JOHN. I'm a one-eyed monster. *(He puts on a mask with one large, glaring eye in the middle of his forehead.)*

(GEORGE, JOE, SANDRA, FRED, ANNA, and MABEL, all about the same age as the others, enter. They stop, stunned by what they see.)

PETE *(roaring)*. Hey, what are you doing here?

JOE. That's Pete—I know his voice.

PETE. I'm a dragon. Get lost.

GEORGE. Aw, he's sore because we won the game.

SANDRA. Where'd they get those masks?

JOE *(picking up a mask from the floor)*. This is a troll!

GEORGE. They took the best ones.

ALICE. Leave those alone. They're not yours.

SANDRA. They're not yours, either. *(She picks up a tiger mask.)* I'm going to be a tiger.

PETE *(snatching it away from her)*. Nothing doing. You take the trolls. We're the monsters.

SANDRA. Trolls! They're those funny little people that live under bridges. *(to PETE)* But maybe I'd like to be a dragon.

PETE *(roaring)*. I'm the dragon, and you're in my power. Get that troll mask on, or *I'll eat you.*

JOE *(putting on a troll mask)*. Who's afraid? I'm a troll . . . watch me. *(He does some squatty dance steps.)*

MABEL *(frightened)*. I don't know who these kids are. I

don't want to play this game.

FRED.   Who wants to be a troll?

JOE.   We've got to defend ourselves. Trolls can stick to-gether.

ANNA.   But they're *monsters.*

GEORGE.   Trolls can't fight monsters.

JOE.   Hurry up! Trolls have power, too.

(GEORGE, FRED, ANNA, SANDRA, *and* MABEL *put on troll masks.*)

PETE.   Now, trolls, we have you in our power.

FRED.   Why?

PETE *(roaring, shaking with rage).*   Because I'm a dragon —and I'm magic. These are my monsters *(he gestures to* ALICE, MARTA, *and* JOHN *), and we're going to* DESTROY YOU—ONE BY ONE!

MARTA.   You had a nerve, coming in here.

ALICE.   It's not your house.

JOE.   It's not yours, either.

JOHN.   We're in command here.

PETE.   I'm in command. And we don't like trolls.

ALICE.   We *hate* trolls.

MARTA.   We're going to destroy you.

JOE.   Trolls can come here if they like.

SANDRA.   Trolls can go anywhere.

JOHN.   Trolls live under bridges—that's where you belong.

PETE.   Monsters—ready for attack!

(The monsters, all together, take a step downstage. The trolls, frightened, cluster downstage right. PETE *makes spell-casting gestures.)*

GEORGE.   Think of something, quick!

JOE.   I know, we'll entertain 'em.

(Lively music comes in. Trolls do a brave, thumping, squatty little dance. Monsters roar, come a step closer.)

SANDRA.   Trolls! They don't like our dance.

MABEL.   We better hide . . .

ANNA.   Where?

MABEL.   Where can we hide?

(Monsters step closer, growling, waving their arms.)

JOE *(in low tones meant for trolls alone).*   In the trunk! It's safe in the trunk, until the monsters go to sleep.

FRED.   What if they don't go to sleep?

JOE.   Sh-h-h! Trolls have power, too. Trolls can put monsters to sleep.

(Monsters break into a run, chase trolls around the stage, roaring at them, trolls shrieking. Trolls run faster and faster, keeping just out of reach. Unnoticed by the monsters, JOE *scampers offstage right. The rest of the trolls run to the trunk, jump in. Monsters slam the lid*

down on them, laugh and shout in triumph, thinking
they have won. Trolls beat and kick from the inside.
JOE *appears, stands at the edge of the stage, makes*
spell-casting gestures. Sleep music comes in softly.)

PETE *(roaring).* Silence in there! *(to* JOHN*)* One-Eye,
guard the prisoners. *(*JOHN *sits on top of the trunk, arms*
folded.)

JOE *(in low tones, like a hypnotist).* Monsters, you're getting very sleepy. Soon you'll be asleep.

(The monsters begin to stretch and yawn.)

ALICE. Oh, I'm tired. Trolls wear you out.

MARTA. We'll have to take a rest. Guard them well, One-
Eye.

JOHN *(yawning).* Have no fear.

(Monsters collapse at left, heaving, sighing, fall asleep.
JOHN *dozes off on top of the trunk, his head dropping*
slowly on his chest. Sleep music plays soothingly. JOE
stands watching the sleeping monsters.)

JOE. Monsters are stronger, but trolls are smarter. Those
guys will wake up pretty soon. I've got to figure out a
way to get their masks off, somehow. You take off the
mask to break the spell. *(He ponders, has an idea, jumps*
up and down in glee.) That's it! I know what to do.

*(*JOE *runs offstage. The monsters snore loudly.* JOE
comes back, tiptoeing, carrying three or four long

broomstraws fastened together to make a tickler. He crosses to where PETE *lies sleeping, tickles his dragon nose with the broomstraw.* PETE *sneezes, goes on sleeping.* JOE *laughs to himself, then slips the straws under* PETE's *mask, tickles his face.* PETE *jumps up with a roar, snatches the mask off, stands in amazement, scratching his face.* JOE *jumps up and down, laughing.)*

PETE.   What—who are you?

(JOE *puts a finger to his lips, tickles* MARTA *under her werewolf mask.* MARTA *jumps up in alarm, snatches off her mask, scratches her nose.)*

MARTA.   Catch that mouse! Where did it go?

(JOE *puts his finger to his lips, tickles* ALICE *under her bat mask. She jumps up, shrieking, tearing off her mask.)*

ALICE.   I think a cat attacked me.

MARTA.   I think it was a lion.

JOE *(doubled up with laughter).*   People again! My, you look better! *(There are sounds of kicking and beating and muffled cries from the trunk.* JOE *runs over to it.)* Coming, friends.

PETE.   What's in there?

JOE.   Trolls. Don't you remember?

PETE.   Trolls! That's right—we chased 'em in.

JOE.   Don't be alarmed. They just want to get out. *(He tickles* JOHN *under his mask.* JOHN *jumps to the floor with a loud cry, tears off his mask.)*

JOHN. A man needs two eyes to defend himself. Who's attacking me? *(He looks all around him.* JOE *doubles up again.)* What's so funny?

*(*JOE *quickly opens the trunk. The trolls jump out, cheer, run about, stretching, breathing deeply.)*

MABEL. Whew! That's enough of that.

SANDRA. It was suffocating in there. *(She falls to the floor, fainting. Trolls gather around, slapping her wrists, talking to her anxiously.)*

GEORGE. Sandra—what's wrong?

JOE. Oh, help! She's fainted. Stand back—give her air.

ALICE *(kneeling beside* SANDRA *).* Get that mask off, quick —she can't breathe through it.

*(*ALICE *and* MARTA *take* SANDRA's *mask off. Everybody waits anxiously.)*

MABEL. There wasn't any air in that old trunk. *(She removes her mask.)*

GEORGE. You can't breathe very well through a mask. *(He removes his mask.)*

ANNA. Right. They're unhealthy.

JOHN. You shouldn't ever play in a trunk. My pop says its dangerous.

FRED. Yeah. I knew a kid got killed that way. *(He removes his mask.)*

ANNA *(looking accusingly at the monsters).* They made us do it.

ALICE *(moving* SANDRA'S *arms).* What'll we do?

GEORGE. Get a doctor.

PETE. Aw, she's all right. *(nudging* SANDRA *roughly)* Wake up, troll!

ALICE. Leave her alone, Pete!

*(*SANDRA *stirs, opens her eyes. They watch breathlessly.)*

ANNA. She's coming to!

SANDRA *(sitting up).* What happened?

ALICE. You fainted.

MABEL. Are you all right?

SANDRA *(breathing deeply).* I guess so. *(All sigh with relief.* ALICE *and* MABEL *hug* SANDRA.*)* I'm glad to get that old mask off.

ALICE *(to* PETE*).* You better be glad she's okay. It was all your fault.

PETE. What do you mean? You were in on it, too.

ALICE. You made us fight the trolls.

MARTA. And hold 'em prisoner in the trunk.

ALICE. Sandra might have smothered. You're a monster!

JOHN. We were all monsters.

ALICE. Not any more. I couldn't stand being a bat! *(She hurls her mask into a corner.)* I thought it would be fun— but it wasn't me.

MARTA. I hate werewolves! *(She hurls her mask after* ALICE'S.)

PETE. We had magic power, we were winning!

MARTA. Trolls had more, they put us to sleep.

MABEL. Forget it, nobody won.

JOE *(smiling).* But I like being a troll!

GEORGE *(to* JOE). Hey, you've still got your mask on. *(All turn to look at* JOE.) Take it off, Joe.

JOE. No, I won't!

JOHN. Yes, you will. We took ours off.

> *(They swoop down on* JOE, *who dances teasingly away, dodging them. They close in on him.* GEORGE *rips* JOE's *mask off as he howls in protest.* PETE *is standing aside, downcast.)*

JOE. Hey, give that back. Give me back my mask.

GEORGE *(throwing it in the corner with the others).* You can't like anybody with a mask on.

PETE. You're all chicken.

JOHN. So you want to be a dragon all the time?

GEORGE. You want to win? That mask made you a loser, man.

MARTA. He's bad enough without it.

JOHN. Knock it off. He's okay without it.

JOE. Let's go play stickball.

ALICE.   Put away the stuff first.

>*(They put the masks and bits of costumes back in the trunk, give the lid a final slam. PETE is standing glumly alone at the edge of the stage. They hurry out the way they came, talking about the game.)*

GEORGE.   I saw some new kids out there playing . . .

JOHN.   Are they good?

GEORGE.   They look good. We'll take 'em on.

>*(PETE is left alone on stage for a moment. Then JOHN returns.)*

JOHN.   Hey, dragon! You coming?

PETE *(happily, runs toward him)*.   Don't call me that anymore. I'm just me. *(JOHN puts his arm around PETE as they go off together.)*

Playing time: 10 minutes.

PRODUCTION NOTES

This play needs a few bits of costumes, crowns, a scepter, masks, and a trunk. Masks can be made for monsters and trolls out of papier-mâché, with painted features, or you can use brown paper bags. Be sure to cut large holes for eyes (One-Eye's real eye openings can be disguised, with his large eye painted in the middle) and mouths, so that the mask will not keep the audience from hearing you speak your lines. Pictures of trolls can be found in books of Norwegian folk tales.

If the play is fully staged, a large box can be built as a frame, upstage center, covered with cardboard or heavy paper painted to look like a trunk. The back can be left open to make it more comfortable for the actors inside. If you want to do it simply in your school room, the trunk can be improvised with chairs, covered with a sheet or a curtain.

There are good recordings of Edvard Grieg's "Peer Gynt Suite" available. You can select music from it that is especially suited to the trolls' dance as well as to the opening of the play.

AUTOMA

In our fast-changing world, schools are trying many new methods. You might have known that the computer would come into your classrooms sooner or later. Teaching machines have arrived.

Scientists developed the computer through many stages, starting with the old adding machine. It is now a kind of electronic bank where all sorts of facts can be stored and used whenever they are needed. It is taking over dull and tiring jobs. Many educators believe that it is helping children to read, work math problems faster, and remember the lessons better. The computer does not grow tired. It can slow down for a child who needs more time, and speed up for one who learns faster. It costs a great deal of money, but a machine can never take the place of human teachers. It can help only when a teacher works along with the child who uses it.

There is danger in man's use of the machines he has made. He sometimes forgets that one person is more important than all the computers on earth. In our time, we are finding out that great programs for masses of people may not be good for every human being and his family. The computer can never be greater than those who use it. It cannot dream or create for us, or tell us what is right and wrong. It cannot feel or love or be glad or sorry. Like any other tool man uses, it can be helpful if he remembers he is in control.

The play that follows, AUTOMA, shows how some children and their teachers learn what the computer can and cannot do, and how to make it serve them without taking over their lives.

AUTOMA	BILL
VICKI	MIMI
MARK	SAM
MISS EMERY, a teacher	LIZA
MR. FRANKLIN, a teacher	ELSIE
PROGO, a mechano	RENA
DATA, a mechano	JERRY
NED	ELLEN

(The scene is a schoolroom. Seated at a desk at left are PROGO *and* DATA, *wearing gray jumpsuits marked all over to look like holes in a computer card. They move stiffly; their voices are polite and cold. They never smile. The desk is piled high with rolls of paper, the kind used in teaching typewriters. At right the children are seated at small tables, working math problems. At center are two teaching typewriters.* MISS EMERY *and* MR. FRANKLIN, *the teachers, are helping. They are large, warm, comfortable people.* VICKI *and* MARK *are seated at the typewriters.)*

AUTOMA *(a deep voice from offstage, speaking slowly, in dead tones).* Please type your first name. *(*VICKI *and* MARK *type.)*

VICKI. V - i - c - k - i — Vicki.

MARK. M - a - r - k — Mark.

AUTOMA. Thank you. This is a lesson in addition. If Jane had twelve cookies and her mother put five away, how many cookies did she have left?

MARK. Too many. Made her sick!

VICKI *(counting on her fingers, types).* Eight cookies.

(Colored lights flash on a backdrop.)

AUTOMA. No. Try again.

(VICKI *and* MARK *type.* MARK *pulls* VICKI's *hair.*)

MARK *(to* VICKI*).* Don't count on your fingers.

(VICKI *yells, reaches over, snatches paper from the roll in* MARK's *typewriter, throws it on the floor, stamps on it.* MARK *jumps up, grabs* VICKI *by the shoulders, shakes her.* MISS EMERY *comes over to them, separates them.*)

MISS EMERY. Vicki, Mark, you're always fighting. Get back to work now.

MARK. Vicki ruined my lesson.

VICKI. Mark pulled my hair.

MISS EMERY. Let's start over.

(*Lights flash, bell rings.*)

AUTOMA. Time is up. The answer is seven. Try again.

MARK. Automa won't ever stop, Miss Emery.

VICKI. Automa goes too fast.

MR. FRANKLIN *(to the mechanos).* Progo, can't you get Automa to go more slowly?

PROGO. Yes, of course. But not until Data and I go through yesterday's input.

(*He points to the pile of paper rolls.*)

MARK. Automa is a stupid old machine.

DATA. Automa is not stupid. You must pay attention. Then you will learn.

PROGO.   Keep working with the typewriters.

VICKI.   I can't work mine without Mr. Franklin.

MARK.   I can't work mine without Miss Emery.

NED *(at the table)*.   I can't work 'em at all.

> *(A bell rings.* PROGO *and* DATA *whisper together.)*

MISS EMERY.   Mr. Franklin and I have to go to Class 4 now.

BILL *(at the table)*.   Can't we go to the gym?

OTHER CHILDREN.   Yeah, yeah!

PROGO *(rising)*.   Not yet. We have an idea to speed up the lessons.

DATA *(to the teachers)*.   We'll have something to show you when you come back next period.

MR. FRANKLIN.   Okay, kids, stay and do your best.

> *(The teachers go off right, the children howling in protest.)*

MIMI.   That's not fair.

SAM.   It's our time to go to the gym.

OTHER CHILDREN.   Yeah, yeah.
We're tired.   *(All speak at once.)*
It's time to go.

DATA.   You must be patient, children.

PROGO.   Automa is going to make your reading easy, and your math.

VICKI.   I don't like math, Progo.

MARK.   You can't do it, that's why!

VICKI *(to* PROGO*)*.   Make him stop picking on me.

PROGO.   Automa will help you to like each other.

MARK.   Yeah? *(He laughs scornfully.)* I can't wait!

ELSIE.   Automa is nothing but an old machine.

DATA.   Automa is a great teacher.

SAM.   I'd rather have Miss Emery and Mr. Franklin.

PROGO.   We're starting a new program. First we must clear the desk.

JERRY.   We'll help you clear the desk!

OTHER CHILDREN.   Yeah, yeah.
We'll help you.   *(All speak at once.)*
Everybody help.

(The children rush to the desk, pick up the papers, run around the room, throwing them in the air, shouting. PROGO and DATA vainly try to stop them.)

PROGO.   Children, children—stop at once!

DATA.   You'll only have to wait longer.

ELLEN.   The desk is cleared, why do we have to wait longer? *(She holds papers out of reach of DATA's hand.)*

PROGO.   Stop it, everybody. Stand still where you are.

(The children stop and wait. A loud rumbling noise is heard.)

LIZA.   What's that?

PROGO.   That's Automa.

JERRY.   What's wrong?

DATA.   Automa is hungry—ready for more material.

ELSIE.   Maybe Automa will break down.

117

ELLEN.   Goody, goody! *(The children cheer.)*

DATA.   Maybe we could just go ahead.

(PROGO *looks at her, nods, goes off left. There is a sound of keys being punched, something like a cash register.)*

DATA.   Children, we're going to try an experiment. Instead of feeding your lessons and answers to Automa, we're going to program *you.*

MARK.   You mean—feed *us* to Automa?

DATA.   Exactly. It will save us all time.

MIMI *(frightened)*.   Oh, no, you don't!

LIZA.   I'm not going inside that machine.

OTHER CHILDREN.   No, no!
                  Neither am I.   *(All speak at once.)*
                  Forget it.

DATA.   You'll come out knowing all your lessons—you'll behave better . . .

LIZA.   I don't want to behave. I don't like school, anyhow.

DATA.   You'll be programmed to like your school. You'll be very happy. *(She does not smile.)*

DATA *(continuing, gathers up papers and puts them in a trash basket)*.   We can do away with papers. You won't need any more written tests.

(PROGO *returns.)*

PROGO.   Automa is all set. Automa is programmed for a funhouse.

MIMI. A funhouse! That's different.

JERRY. Man, I'm ready.

ELSIE. But how can it be fun in there?

PROGO. We'll let Automa tell you. Listen to this. *(He goes offstage, punches a key. Lights flash on upstage backdrop.)* Are you ready, Automa?

AUTOMA *(after a slight pause)*. Yes, thank you. Please punch the key for each child's name and number. *(There is a punching sound.)* Come inside, children. You will all have fun. Get your chocolate malted at the door.

ELLEN. Chocolate malted—wow!

(The children file off up left, all but ELSIE, who hangs back.)

ELSIE. No—no. I don't want to go in there.

JERRY. Aw, come on, Elsie, don't be chicken.

ELSIE. I think it's time for our teachers to come back.

(She runs to the right, peers off. DATA takes her firmly by the hand; PROGO comes to the other side.)

DATA. They'll be back very soon. Come along, so you'll be all ready for them.

PROGO. You're going to have lots of fun. *(He does not smile.)*

ELSIE *(shrieking)*. No—no—no . . .

(But PROGO and DATA rush her quickly up and offstage left.)

AUTOMA. Hello, children. Isn't this fun? You're going to have fun—remember—fun.

(There are sounds of hollow cymbals clanging, music, cheers, applause, grating noises, party horns, and a big echoing voice saying "FUN—Fun—fun—" softer, softer, then out. PROGO *and* DATA *return, stand watching flashing lights. Then* MR. FRANKLIN *and* MISS EMERY *return from right.)*

PROGO. Come in, come in. The children are almost ready.

MR. FRANKLIN *(looking around).* But where are they?

PROGO. They're being programmed. They're almost ready . . .

MR. FRANKLIN *(in horror).* Children—being programmed?

DATA. For reading skills, math skills, and behavior.

PROGO. They'll be so different; you won't know them.

MISS EMERY. Progo, you're chilling my blood.

(There is a burst of static, mechanical music comes in. The CHILDREN *file on in perfect step, stand in a rigid line. They are now dressed in gray jumpsuits like the ones* PROGO *and* DATA *wear. They carry huge computer cards and read from them in dead voices. They do not seem to recognize* MISS EMERY *and* MR. FRANKLIN.)*

PROGO. Now—let's see how our experiment has worked out. We'll try reading first. Which ones were having the most trouble with reading?

MISS EMERY. Ned, Ellen, and Sam.

PROGO. All right, Ned, you read for us first.

*(*NED *steps forward one step, reads from his card with ease, but in dead tones.)*

NED.   Some children have more accidents more often than others.

DATA.   Now, Ellen.

ELLEN *(stepping out, reads in the same way).*   Children who run and jump and take chances are more likely to get hurt.

PROGO.   And Sam.

SAM *(stepping out, reads in the same way).*   But no one wants to sit still all the time. We must all remember to be more careful of accidents when we are running and playing.

MISS EMERY.   Good heavens! They sound like Automa.

DATA.   Yes! It's a lot better and faster than before.

MR. FRANKLIN.   Ned, what did that mean, what you just read to me?

NED *(staring blankly in front of him).*   Some children have accidents more often than others.

MR. FRANKLIN.   What does it mean, Sam? Have you had an accident lately?

SAM.   No one wants to sit still all the time.

MISS EMERY.   Ellen, do you get hurt easily?

ELLEN.   Children who run and jump and take chances . . .

PROGO.   They're reading much faster . . .

MISS EMERY.   But they don't understand a word they're saying.

DATA. You people are never satisfied. Let's try the math. Mark, tell us what you learned.

MARK *(stepping forward, announces in dead tones)*. Miss Emery placed fifteen books on her bookshelf. Later she added seven more. Miss Emery placed twenty-two books on the shelf.

MISS EMERY. What if I added six more, Mark? How many would there be?

MARK *(staring blankly in front of him)*. Miss Emery placed twenty-two books on the shelf.

VICKI *(stepping forward)*. Bill weighs sixty-five pounds. His brother weighs forty-five pounds. Bill weighs twenty pounds more than his brother.

MR. FRANKLIN. What if his brother loses five pounds, Vicki? How much more will Bill weigh?

VICKI. Bill weighs sixty-five pounds. His brother . . .

DATA. You are confusing them, Mr. Franklin.

MR. FRANKLIN. Not at all, Data. They simply don't know what they're talking about.

DATA. That's as far as the programming went. You're trying to jump ahead.

PROGO. Mimi, tell us what you learned in your math lesson.

MIMI *(stepping forward, holds up a computer card, speaks in dead tones)*. This punched card is necessary for proper recording. If you have a ten-year-old child, please return it with your remittance in the box that is circled for further information.

(The teachers stare at PROGO *and* DATA.*)*

MR. FRANKLIN.   What on earth is that about?

DATA *(hesitating).*   It's possible a wrong key was punched. We'll send her back for re-programming.

MISS EMERY.   Oh, no you won't. Nobody's going back.

DATA.   Vicki and Mark have learned to like each other.

VICKI *(stepping forward, speaks in dead tones).*   Mark is very nice.

MARK *(stepping forward, in dead tones).*   I get along with Vicki very well.

PROGO.   They have all learned good behavior. Children, tell your teachers what this means.

RENA *(stepping out, speaks in slow rhythm).*   I put the chalk on the chalkboard rack.

JERRY *(following).*   I clean the chalkboard with a dampened sponge.

ELSIE.   I hang my coat on the coatroom hook.

BILL.   I take my place in the lunchroom line.

NED.   I wait my turn on the parallel bars.

ALL THE CHILDREN *(together).*   I put the chalk on the chalkboard rack—I clean the chalkboard with a dampened sponge—I hang my coat on the coatroom hook—I take my place in the lunchroom line—I wait my turn on the parallel bars . . .

MISS EMERY *(stopping her ears).*   Oh, please, that's quite enough! This is dreadful—they aren't people anymore.

PROGO. Yes, they are. They've been programmed, that's all.

DATA. They will grow up to be very successful in science and business.

PROGO. They will own their own automas some day, and program other people.

MR. FRANKLIN. And what do you call such people?

DATA. Automa-tons. There'll be lots of them. Finally everybody will . . .

MR. FRANKLIN. No, impossible! What happens to love and joy and people learning from mistakes?

MISS EMERY. Children, did you like what happened to you in there?

CHILDREN *(in dead voices).* Yes, we liked it.

DATA. You had fun, didn't you?

CHILDREN. Yes, we had fun.

(MISS EMERY *begins to cry.)*

PROGO. Remember, they are just beginning. Bring them back to us regularly, and they will learn more and more correct answers.

MR. FRANKLIN. But will they ever know what the answers mean?

PROGO. That's beside the point, as long as they learn to use them.

DATA. Now, you must treat them with great care until these changes become set.

PROGO.   There must be no noise, no disturbance, no touching.

MR. FRANKLIN.   No noise?

MISS EMERY.   No touching?

PROGO.   Absolutely none.

MR. FRANKLIN *(shouting)*.   You heard that, Miss Emery? All we need is noise, disturbance, touching—TENDER LOVING CARE!

> *(*MR. FRANKLIN *lets out a warwhoop,* MISS EMERY *claps her hands, beats on the desk, cheers. They run to the line of children and begin to push them about, tussling with them noisily and happily. The children draw away in fright, crying out in a shrill chorus.)*

CHILDREN.   Do not clip, fold, staple, or mutilate—
Do not clip, fold, staple, or mutilate . . .

PROGO.   Careful, please. You'll undo all our programming.

MR. FRANKLIN.   Are you sure? That's great!

> *(The* TEACHERS *hug the children, shake them, talk to them, call them by name, pull off their jumpsuits. Finally the children begin to laugh and shove and talk back.* PROGO *and* DATA *go and sit in a corner, stiff and silent.)*

MR. FRANKLIN.   Come on, Jerry, wrestle, man. That's it—that's more like it.

MISS EMERY.   Here, Ellen, let me help you get that tight suit off.

MR. FRANKLIN.   Deep breaths, now, everybody.

(MR. FRANKLIN leads them in deep breaths. He pushes them gently around. Everybody begins to push and laugh. MR. FRANKLIN turns a somersault. The CHILDREN begin to turn somersaults. MISS EMERY starts a game of tag. All is wild and happy confusion. MR. FRANKLIN lets the boys pile on top of him. He gets up, shaking them off. NED is sitting on his shoulders. MARK pulls VICKI's hair. She screams, starts hitting him. MISS EMERY separates them, laughing.)

MISS EMERY. Mark! Vicki! Don't you remember how you learned to get along? Never mind, we'll settle this one later, on the playground.

MR. FRANKLIN *(gently quieting them all)*. There, now. We have our children back again. Lucky we didn't have an accident—all this running and jumping. What was that about accidents, Ned?

NED *(blankly)*. What accidents?

MISS EMERY. Vicki, how many pounds does Bill's brother weigh?

BILL *(blankly)*. I don't have any brother!

PROGO. I told you to handle them carefully.

MR. FRANKLIN. It doesn't matter. Our way is slower, but it works better.

PROGO. You don't understand our system.

DATA. We'll have the truck pick up Automa and the typewriters.

MISS EMERY. Oh, don't do that—we might keep Automa.

MR. FRANKLIN.   The typewriters help on drills and records.

MISS EMERY.   They take over when we're tired. They save us time.

MR. FRANKLIN.   But they're expensive. I think they cost more than we do.

MISS EMERY.   The truth is, Vicki doesn't learn the same way Mark does.

VICKI.   Thank goodness! *(MARK lunges at her; they stop him, laughing.)*

MR. FRANKLIN.   Ned doesn't learn the same way Liza does.

MISS EMERY.   No. Each one is different, and we like it that way.

MR. FRANKLIN.   We love our children.

PROGO.   You'd rather do it the hard way?

TEACHERS and CHILDREN *(in resounding chorus).*   Yes!

MR. FRANKLIN.   Let's have a WELCOME HOME party.

MISS EMERY.   Great! I'll order ice cream.

   (The CHILDREN cheer.)

PROGO.   I guess we'll be going.

MARK.   Say, I've got an idea, Progo.

PROGO.   We don't have much time . . .

MARK.   Why don't we feed you and Data to Automa?

   (The CHILDREN clap and cheer.)

BILL *(moving a step toward the mechanos).* Well, aren't you about ready to be programmed again?

MIMI *(taking a step toward them).* Right. You have to keep on doing it to stay the way you are.

PROGO. Oh, no! We work this out with central control.

(The mechanos move left, a little frightened. The CHILDREN *crowd in on them.)*

DATA. We'll say good-bye—and wish success to everybody.

(The CHILDREN *follow them left.)*

CHILDREN. Don't go yet—
         There's still time—   *(All speak at once.)*
         We could try . . .

*(*PROGO *and* DATA *go quickly off left, almost running. The* TEACHERS *are laughing. The* CHILDREN *return to them.)*

MISS EMERY. What kind of ice cream?

CHILDREN *(very quickly).* Chocolate.
                       Pistachio.
                       Black raspberry.
                       Fudge ripple.
                       Cherry.
                       Maple nut.
                       Butter pecan.
                       Strawberry.

MISS EMERY. Please! Do I have to get Automa to decide?

CHILDREN *(in chorus).* No! No! No!

ELSIE.   Let it be a surprise.

(The CHILDREN *cheer.)*

Playing time: 15 minutes.

PRODUCTION NOTES

Costumes and props for AUTOMA can be improvised easily. There are many one-piece garments that can serve as jumpsuits. If possible, they should be gray, or a quiet color that doesn't suggest much life. The black marks resembling computer-punched holes can be put on with burnt cork if you want them to wash out later, or pieces of black "iron-on" tape can be used. Sound effects can be taped if a recorder is available. If not, you can figure out ways to make "live noises" offstage. If possible, Automa's voice should be amplified by having the actor speak over a microphone. If there is an echo, it will help.

The flashing of colored lights is created in many different ways, depending on what kind of lighting you have in your theater or auditorium. One of the simplest ways is to move flashlights covered with colored gels quickly in circles. Another is to set up a spotlight focused on the upstage wall and fasten a larger wheel just in front of the lens. Then tape colored gels in pie-shaped pieces around the wheel, so that when you spin it around, the different colors flash on the wall. Gels are sheets of colored gelatine used for stage lighting. They can be bought in theatrical supply stores, or perhaps your school or a theater may have some on hand.

Office typewriters will serve for teaching machines, or you can cover them with a cardboard casing painted gray to look more like the larger teaching typewriters. Pictures of these can be found in books on computers.